D0099327

THE COLLECTED POEMS OF DYLAN THOMAS

821.91

THE
COLLECTED
POEMS
OF
DYLAN
THOMAS

SONORA HIGH SCHOOL
LIBRARY

A NEW DIRECTIONS BOOK

9141

Copyright 1939, 1942, 1946 by New Directions.
Copyright 1952, 1953 by Dylan Thomas.
©1957 by New Directions

All rights reserved. Except for brief passages quoted in a
newspaper, magazine, radio, or television review, no part of
this book may be reproduced in any form or by any means,
electronic or mechanical, including photocopying and re-
cording, or by any information storage and retrieval
system, without permission in writing from the Publisher.

Frontispiece photograph by Marion Morehouse.

New Directions Books are published for James Laughlin
by New Directions Publishing Corporation,
333 Sixth Avenue, New York 10014

TWENTY-FIRST PRINTING

CONTENTS

to
Caitlin

NOTE

The prologue in verse, written for this collected edition of my poems, is intended as an address to my readers, the strangers.

This book contains most of the poems I have written, and all, up to the present year, that I wish to preserve. Some of them I have revised a little, but if I went on revising everything that I now do not like in this book I should be so busy that I would have no time to try to write new poems.

I read somewhere of a shepherd who, when asked why he made, from within fairy rings, ritual observances to the moon to protect his flocks, replied: 'I'd be a damn' fool if I didn't!' These poems, with all their crudities, doubts, and confusions, are written for the love of Man and in praise of God, and I'd be a damn' fool if they weren't.

DYLAN THOMAS

This day winding down now
At God speeded summer's end
In the torrent salmon sun,
In my seashaken house
On a breakneck of rocks
Tangled with chirrup and fruit,
Froth, flute, fin and quill
At a wood's dancing hoof,
By scummed, starfish sands
With their fishwife cross
Gulls, pipers, cockles, and sails,
Out there, crow black, men
Tackled with clouds, who kneel
To the sunset nets,
Geese nearly in heaven, boys
Stabbing, and herons, and shells
That speak seven seas,
Eternal waters away
From the cities of nine
Days' night whose towers will catch
In the religious wind
Like stalks of tall, dry straw,
At poor peace I sing
To you strangers (though song
Is a burning and crested act,
The fire of birds in

The world's turning wood,
For my sawn, splay sounds),
Out of these seathumbed leaves
That will fly and fall
Like leaves of trees and as soon
Crumble and undie
Into the dogdayed night.
Seaward the salmon, sucked sun slips,
And the dumb swans drub blue
My dabbed bay's dusk, as I hack
This rumpus of shapes
For you to know
How I, a spinning man,
Glory also this star, bird
Roared, sea born, man torn, blood blest.
Hark: I trumpet the place,
From fish to jumping hill! Look:
I build my bellowing ark
To the best of my love
As the flood begins,
Out of the fountainhead
Of fear, rage red, manalive,
Molten and mountainous to stream
Over the wound asleep
Sheep white hollow farms

To Wales in my arms.
Hoo, there, in castle keep,
You king singsong owls, who moonbeam
The flickering runs and dive
The dingle furred deer dead!
Huloo, on plumbed bryns,
O my ruffled ring dove
In the hooting, nearly dark
With Welsh and reverent rook,
Coo rooing the woods' praise,
Who moons her blue notes from her nest
Down to the curlew herd!
Ho, hullaballoing clan
Agape, with woe
In your beaks, on the gabbing capes!
Heigh, on horseback hill, jack
Whisking hare! who
Hears, there, this fox light, my flood ship's
Clangour as I hew and smite
(A clash of anvils for my
Hubbub and fiddle, this tune
On a tongued puffball)
But animals thick as thieves
On God's rough tumbling grounds
(Hail to His beasthood!).
Beasts who sleep good and thin,

Hist, in hogsback woods! The haystacked
Hollow farms in a throng
Of waters cluck and cling,
And barnroofs cockcrow war!
O kingdom of neighbours, finned
Felled and quilled, flash to my patch
Work ark and the moonshine
Drinking Noah of the bay,
With pelt, and scale, and fleece:
Only the drowned deep bells
Of sheep and churches noise
Poor peace as the sun sets
And dark shoals every holy field.
We will ride out alone, and then,
Under the stars of Wales,
Cry, Multitudes of arks! Across
The water lidded lands,
Manned with their loves they'll move,
Like wooden islands, hill to hill.
Huloo, my prowed dove with a flute!
Ahoy, old, sea-legged fox,
Tom tit and Dai mouse!
My ark sings in the sun
At God speeded summer's end
And the flood flowers now.

THE COLLECTED POEMS OF DYLAN THOMAS

I

I see the boys of summer in their ruin
Lay the gold tithings barren,
Setting no store by harvest, freeze the soils;
There in their heat the winter floods
Of frozen loves they fetch their girls,
And drown the cargoed apples in their tides.

These boys of light are curdlers in their folly,
Sour the boiling honey;
The jacks of frost they finger in the hives;
There in the sun the frigid threads
Of doubt and dark they feed their nerves;
The signal moon is zero in their voids.

I see the summer children in their mothers
Split up the brawned womb's weathers,
Divide the night and day with fairy thumbs;
There in the deep with quartered shades
Of sun and moon they paint their dams
As sunlight paints the shelling of their heads.

I see that from these boys shall men of nothing
Stature by seedy shifting,
Or lame the air with leaping from its heats;
There from their hearts the dogdayed pulse
Of love and light bursts in their throats.
O see the pulse of summer in the ice.

But seasons must be challenged or they totter
Into a chiming quarter
Where, punctual as death, we ring the stars;
There, in his night, the black-tongued bells
The sleepy man of winter pulls,
Nor blows back moon-and-midnight as she blows.

We are the dark deniers, let us summon
Death from a summer woman,
A muscling life from lovers in their cramp,
From the fair dead who flush the sea
The bright-eyed worm on Davy's lamp,
And from the planted womb the man of straw.

We summer boys in this four-winded spinning,
Green of the seaweeds' iron,
Hold up the noisy sea and drop her birds,
Pick the world's ball of wave and froth
To choke the deserts with her tides,
And comb the county gardens for a wreath.

In spring we cross our foreheads with the holly,
Heigh ho the blood and berry,
And nail the merry squires to the trees;
Here love's damp muscle dries and dies,
Here break a kiss in no love's quarry.
O see the poles of promise in the boys.

III

I see you boys of summer in your ruin.
Man in his maggot's barren.
And boys are full and foreign in the pouch.
I am the man your father was.
We are the sons of flint and pitch.
O see the poles are kissing as they cross.

When once the twilight locks no longer
Locked in the long worm of my finger
Nor damned the sea that sped about my fist,
The mouth of time sucked, like a sponge,
The milky acid on each hinge,
And swallowed dry the waters of the breast.

When the galactic sea was sucked
And all the dry seabed unlocked,
I sent my creature scouting on the globe,
That globe itself of hair and bone
That, sewn to me by nerve and brain,
Had stringed my flask of matter to his rib.

My fuses timed to charge his heart,
He blew like powder to the light
And held a little sabbath with the sun,
But when the stars, assuming shape,
Drew in his eyes the straws of sleep,
He drowned his father's magics in a dream.

All issue armoured, of the grave,
The redhaired cancer still alive,
The cataracted eyes that filmed their cloth;
Some dead undid their bushy jaws,
And bags of blood let out their flies;
He had by heart the Christ-cross-row of death.

Sleep navigates the tides of time;
The dry Sargasso of the tomb
Gives up its dead to such a working sea;
And sleep rolls mute above the beds
Where fishes' food is fed the shades
Who periscope through flowers to the sky.

When once the twilight screws were turned,
And mother milk was stiff as sand,
I sent my own ambassador to light;
By trick or chance he fell asleep
And conjured up a carcass shape
To rob me of my fluids in his heart.

Awake, my sleeper, to the sun,
A worker in the morning town,
And leave the poppied pickthank where he lies;
The fences of the light are down,
All but the briskest riders thrown,
And worlds hang on the trees.

A process in the weather of the heart
Turns damp to dry; the golden shot
Storms in the freezing tomb.
A weather in the quarter of the veins
Turns night to day; blood in their suns
Lights up the living worm.

A process in the eye forwarns
The bones of blindness; and the womb
Drives in a death as life leaks out.

A darkness in the weather of the eye
Is half its light; the fathomed sea
Breaks on unangled land.
The seed that makes a forest of the loin
Forks half its fruit; and half drops down,
Slow in a sleeping wind.

A weather in the flesh and bone
Is damp and dry; the quick and dead
Move like two ghosts before the eye.

A process in the weather of the world
Turns ghost to ghost; each mothered child
Sits in their double shade.
A process blows the moon into the sun,
Pulls down the shabby curtains of the skin;
And the heart gives up its dead.

Before I knocked and flesh let enter,
With liquid hands tapped on the womb,
I who was shapeless as the water
That shaped the Jordan near my home
Was brother to Mnetha's daughter
And sister to the fathering worm.

I who was deaf to spring and summer,
Who knew not sun nor moon by name,
Felt thud beneath my flesh's armour,
As yet was in a molten form,
The leaden stars, the rainy hammer
Swung by my father from his dome.

I knew the message of the winter,
The darted hail, the childish snow,
And the wind was my sister suitor;
Wind in me leaped, the hellborn dew;
My veins flowed with the Eastern weather;
Ungotten I knew night and day.

As yet ungotten, I did suffer;
The rack of dreams my lily bones
Did twist into a living cipher,
And flesh was snipped to cross the lines
Of gallow crosses on the liver
And brambles in the wringing brains.

My throat knew thirst before the structure
Of skin and vein around the well
Where words and water make a mixture
Unfailing till the blood runs foul;
My heart knew love, my belly hunger;
I smelt the maggot in my stool.

And time cast forth my mortal creature
To drift or drown upon the seas
Acquainted with the salt adventure
Of tides that never touch the shores.
I who was rich was made the richer
By sipping at the vine of days.

I, born of flesh and ghost, was neither
A ghost nor man, but mortal ghost.
And I was struck down by death's feather.
I was a mortal to the last
Long breath that carried to my father
The message of his dying christ.

You who bow down at cross and altar,
Remember me and pity Him
Who took my flesh and bone for armour
And doublecrossed my mother's womb.

The force that through the green fuse drives the flower
Drives my green age; that blasts the roots of trees
Is my destroyer.
And I am dumb to tell the crooked rose
My youth is bent by the same wintry fever.

The force that drives the water through the rocks
Drives my red blood; that dries the mouthing streams
Turns mine to wax.
And I am dumb to mouth unto my veins
How at the mountain spring the same mouth sucks.

The hand that whirls the water in the pool
Stirs the quicksand; that ropes the blowing wind
Hauls my shroud sail.
And I am dumb to tell the hanging man
How of my clay is made the hangman's lime.

The lips of time leech to the fountain head;
Love drips and gathers, but the fallen blood
Shall calm her sores.
And I am dumb to tell a weather's wind
How time has ticked a heaven round the stars.

And I am dumb to tell the lover's tomb
How at my sheet goes the same crooked worm.

My hero bares his nerves along my wrist
That rules from wrist to shoulder,
Unpacks the head that, like a sleepy ghost,
Leans on my mortal ruler,
The proud spine spurning turn and twist.

And these poor nerves so wired to the skull
Ache on the lovelorn paper
I hug to love with my unruly scrawl
That utters all love hunger
And tells the page the empty ill.

My hero bares my side and sees his heart
Tread, like a naked Venus,
The beach of flesh, and wind her bloodred plait;
Stripping my loin of promise,
He promises a secret heat.

He holds the wire from this box of nerves
Praising the mortal error
Of birth and death, the two sad knaves of thieves,
And the hunger's emperor;
He pulls the chain, the cistern moves.

Where once the waters of your face
Spun to my screws, your dry ghost blows,
The dead turns up its eye;
Where once the mermen through your ice
Pushed up their hair, the dry wind steers
Through salt and root and roe.

Where once your green knots sank their splice
Into the tided cord, there goes
The green unraveller,
His scissors oiled, his knife hung loose
To cut the channels at their source
And lay the wet fruits low.

Invisible, your clocking tides
Break on the lovebeds of the weeds;
The weed of love's left dry;
There round about your stones the shades
Of children go who, from their voids,
Cry to the dolphined sea.

Dry as a tomb, your coloured lids
Shall not be latched while magic glides
Sage on the earth and sky;
There shall be corals in your beds,
There shall be serpents in your tides,
Till all our sea-faiths die.

If I were tickled by the rub of love,
A rooking girl who stole me for her side,
Broke through her straws, breaking my bandaged string,
If the red tickle as the cattle calve
Still set to scratch a laughter from my lung,
I would not fear the apple nor the flood
Nor the bad blood of spring.

Shall it be male or female? say the cells,
And drop the plum like fire from the flesh.
If I were tickled by the hatching hair,
The winging bone that sprouted in the heels,
The itch of man upon the baby's thigh,
I would not fear the gallows nor the axe
Nor the crossed sticks of war.

Shall it be male or female? say the fingers
That chalk the walls with green girls and their men.
I would not fear the muscling-in of love
If I were tickled by the urchin hungers
Rehearsing heat upon a raw-edged nerve.
I would not fear the devil in the loin
Nor the outspoken grave.

If I were tickled by the lovers' rub
That wipes away not crow's-foot nor the lock
Of sick old manhood on the fallen jaws,
Time and the crabs and the sweethearting crib
Would leave me cold as butter for the flies,
The sea of scums could drown me as it broke
Dead on the sweethearts' toes.

This world is half the devil's and my own,
Daft with the drug that's smoking in a girl
And curling round the bud that forks her eye.
An old man's shank one-marrowed with my bone,
And all the herrings smelling in the sea,
I sit and watch the worm beneath my nail
Wearing the quick away.

And that's the rub, the only rub that tickles.
The knobbly ape that swings along his sex
From damp love-darkness and the nurse's twist
Can never raise the midnight of a chuckle,
Nor when he finds a beauty in the breast
Of lover, mother, lovers, or his six
Feet in the rubbing dust.

And what's the rub? Death's feather on the nerve?
Your mouth, my love, the thistle in the kiss?
My Jack of Christ born thorny on the tree?
The words of death are dryer than his stiff,
My wordy wounds are printed with your hair.
I would be tickled by the rub that is:
Man be my metaphor.

I

Our eunuch dreams, all seedless in the light,
Of light and love, the tempers of the heart,
Whack their boys' limbs,
And, winding-footed in their shawl and sheet,
Groom the dark brides, the widows of the night
Fold in their arms.

The shades of girls, all flavoured from their shrouds,
When sunlight goes are sundered from the worm,
The bones of men, the broken in their beds,
By midnight pulleys that unhouse the tomb.

II

In this our age the gunman and his moll,
Two one-dimensioned ghosts, love on a reel,
Strange to our solid eye,
And speak their midnight nothings as they swell;
When cameras shut they hurry to their hole
Down in the yard of day.

They dance between their arclamps and our skull,
Impose their shots, showing the nights away;
We watch the show of shadows kiss or kill,
Flavoured of celluloid give love the lie.

III

Which is the world? Of our two sleepings, which
Shall fall awake when cures and their itch
Raise up this red-eyed earth?
Pack off the shapes of daylight and their starch,
The sunny gentlemen, the Welshing rich,
Or drive the night-geared forth.

The photograph is married to the eye,
Grafts on its bride one-sided skins of truth;
The dream has sucked the sleeper of his faith
That shrouded men might marrow as they fly.

IV

This is the world: the lying likeness of
Our strips of stuff that tatter as we move
Loving and being loth;
The dream that kicks the buried from their sack
And lets their trash be honoured as the quick.
This is the world. Have faith.

For we shall be a shouter like the cock,
Blowing the old dead back; our shots shall smack
The image from the plates;
And we shall be fit fellows for a life,

And who remain shall flower as they love,
Praise to our faring hearts.

Especially when the October wind
With frosty fingers punishes my hair,
Caught by the crabbing sun I walk on fire
And cast a shadow crab upon the land,
By the sea's side, hearing the noise of birds,
Hearing the raven cough in winter sticks,
My busy heart who shudders as she talks
Sheds the syllabic blood and drains her words.

Shut, too, in a tower of words, I mark
On the horizon walking like the trees
The wordy shapes of women, and the rows
Of the star-gestured children in the park.
Some let me make you of the vowelled beeches,
Some of the oaken voices, from the roots
Of many a thorny shire tell you notes,
Some let me make you of the water's speeches.

Behind a pot of ferns the wagging clock
Tells me the hour's word, the neural meaning
Flies on the shafted disk, declaims the morning
And tells the windy weather in the cock.
Some let me make you of the meadow's signs;
The signal grass that tells me all I know
Breaks with the wormy winter through the eye.
Some let me tell you of the raven's sins.

Especially when the October wind
(Some let me make you of autumnal spells,
The spider-tongued, and the loud hill of Wales)
With fists of turnips punishes the land,
Some let me make you of the heartless words.
The heart is drained that, spelling in the scurry
Of chemic blood, warned of the coming fury.
By the sea's side hear the dark-vowelled birds.

When, like a running grave, time tracks you down,
Your calm and cuddled is a scythe of hairs,
Love in her gear is slowly through the house,
Up naked stairs, a turtle in a hearse,
Hauled to the dome,

Comes, like a scissors stalking, tailor age,
Deliver me who, timid in my tribe,
Of love am barer than Cadaver's trap
Robbed of the foxy tongue, his footed tape
Of the bone inch,

Deliver me, my masters, head and heart,
Heart of Cadaver's candle waxes thin,
When blood, spade-handed, and the logic time
Drive children up like bruises to the thumb,
From maid and head,

For, sunday faced, with dusters in my glove,
Chaste and the chaser, man with the cockshut eye,
I, that time's jacket or the coat of ice
May fail to fasten with a virgin o
In the straight grave,

Stride through Cadaver's country in my force,
My pickbrain masters morsing on the stone
Despair of blood, faith in the maiden's slime,
Halt among eunuchs, and the nitric stain
On fork and face.

Time is a foolish fancy, time and fool.
No, no, you lover skull, descending hammer
Descends, my masters, on the entered honour.
You hero skull, Cadaver in the hangar
Tells the stick, 'fail.'

Joy is no knocking nation, sir and madam,
The cancer's fusion, or the summer feather
Lit on the cuddled tree, the cross of fever,
Nor city tar and subway bored to foster
Man through macadam.

I damp the waxlights in your tower dome.
Joy is the knock of dust, Cadaver's shoot
Of bud of Adam through his boxy shift,
Love's twilit nation and the skull of state,
Sir, is your doom.

Everything ends, the tower ending and,
(Have with the house of wind), the leaning scene,
Ball of the foot depending from the sun,
(Give, summer, over), the cemented skin,
The actions' end.

All, men my madmen, the unwholesome wind
With whistler's cough contages, time on track
Shapes in a cinder death; love for his trick,
Happy Cadaver's hunger as you take
The kissproof world.

From love's first fever to her plague, from the soft second
And to the hollow minute of the womb,
From the unfolding to the scissored caul,
The time for breast and the green apron age
When no mouth stirred about the hanging famine,
All world was one, one windy nothing,
My world was christened in a stream of milk.
And earth and sky were as one airy hill,
The sun and moon shed one white light.

From the first print of the unshodden foot, the lifting
Hand, the breaking of the hair,
From the first secret of the heart, the warning ghost,
And to the first dumb wonder at the flesh,
The sun was red, the moon was grey,
The earth and sky were as two mountains meeting.

The body prospered, teeth in the marrowed gums,
The growing bones, the rumour of manseed
Within the hallowed gland, blood blessed the heart,
And the four winds, that had long blown as one,
Shone in my ears the light of sound,
Called in my eyes the sound of light.
And yellow was the multiplying sand,
Each golden grain spat life into its fellow,
Green was the singing house.

The plum my mother picked matured slowly,
The boy she dropped from darkness at her side
Into the sided lap of light grew strong,
Was muscled, matted, wise to the crying thigh
And to the voice that, like a voice of hunger,
Itched in the noise of wind and sun.

And from the first declension of the flesh
I learnt man's tongue, to twist the shapes of thoughts
Into the stony idiom of the brain,
To shade and knit anew the patch of words
Left by the dead who, in their moonless acre,
Need no word's warmth.
The root of tongues ends in a spentout cancer,
That but a name, where maggots have their X.

I learnt the verbs of will, and had my secret;
The code of night tapped on my tongue;
What had been one was many sounding minded.

One womb, one mind, spewed out the matter,
One breast gave suck the fever's issue;
From the divorcing sky I learnt the double,
The two-framed globe that spun into a score;
A million minds gave suck to such a bud
As forks my eye;
Youth did condense; the tears of spring
Dissolved in summer and the hundred seasons;
One sun, one manna, warmed and fed.

In the beginning was the three-pointed star,
One smile of light across the empty face;
One bough of bone across the rooting air,
The substance forked that marrowed the first sun;
And, burning ciphers on the round of space,
Heaven and hell mixed as they spun.

In the beginning was the pale signature,
Three-syllabled and starry as the smile;
And after came the imprints on the water,
Stamp of the minted face upon the moon;
The blood that touched the crosstree and the grail
Touched the first cloud and left a sign.

In the beginning was the mounting fire
That set alight the weathers from a spark,
A three-eyed, red-eyed spark, blunt as a flower;
Life rose and spouted from the rolling seas,
Burst in the roots, pumped from the earth and rock
The secret oils that drive the grass.

In the beginning was the word, the word
That from the solid bases of the light
Abstracted all the letters of the void;
And from the cloudy bases of the breath
The word flowed up, translating to the heart
First characters of birth and death.

In the beginning was the secret brain.
The brain was celled and soldered in the thought
Before the pitch was forking to a sun;
Before the veins were shaking in their sieve,
Blood shot and scattered to the winds of light
The ribbed original of love.

Light breaks where no sun shines;
Where no sea runs, the waters of the heart
Push in their tides;
And, broken ghosts with glow-worms in their heads,
The things of light
File through the flesh where no flesh decks the bones.

A candle in the thighs
Warms youth and seed and burns the seeds of age;
Where no seed stirs,
The fruit of man unwrinkles in the stars,
Bright as a fig;
Where no wax is, the candle shows its hairs.

Dawn breaks behind the eyes;
From poles of skull and toe the windy blood
Slides like a sea;
Nor fenced, nor staked, the gushers of the sky
Spout to the rod
Divining in a smile the oil of tears.

Night in the sockets rounds,
Like some pitch moon, the limit of the globes;
Day lights the bone;
Where no cold is, the skinning gales unpin
The winter's robes;
The film of spring is hanging from the lids.

Light breaks on secret lots,
On tips of thought where thoughts smell in the rain;
When logics die,
The secret of the soil grows through the eye,
And blood jumps in the sun;
Above the waste allotments the dawn halts.

I fellowed sleep who kissed me in the brain,
Let fall the tear of time; the sleeper's eye,
Shifting to light, turned on me like a moon.
So, planing-heeled, I flew along my man
And dropped on dreaming and the upward sky.

I fled the earth and, naked, climbed the weather,
Reaching a second ground far from the stars;
And there we wept, I and a ghostly other,
My mothers-eyed, upon the tops of trees;
I fled that ground as lightly as a feather.

'My fathers' globe knocks on its nave and sings.'
'This that we tread was, too, your fathers' land.'
'But this we tread bears the angelic gangs,
Sweet are their fathered faces in their wings.'
'These are but dreaming men. Breathe, and they fade.'

Faded my elbow ghost, the mothers-eyed,
As, blowing on the angels, I was lost
On that cloud coast to each grave-gabbing shade;
I blew the dreaming fellows to their bed
Where still they sleep unknowing of their ghost.

Then all the matter of the living air
Raised up a voice, and, climbing on the words,
I spelt my vision with a hand and hair,
How light the sleeping on this soily star,
How deep the waking in the worlded clouds.

There grows the hours' ladder to the sun,
Each rung a love or losing to the last,
The inches monkeyed by the blood of man.
An old, mad man still climbing in his ghost,
My fathers' ghost is climbing in the rain.

I dreamed my genesis in sweat of sleep, breaking
Through the rotating shell, strong
As motor muscle on the drill, driving
Through vision and the girdered nerve.

From limbs that had the measure of the worm, shuffled
Off from the creasing flesh, filed
Through all the irons in the grass, metal
Of suns in the man-melting night.

Heir to the scalding veins that hold love's drop, costly
A creature in my bones I
Rounded my globe of heritage, journey
In bottom gear through night-geared man.

I dreamed my genesis and died again, shrapnel
Rammed in the marching heart, hole
In the stitched wound and clotted wind, muzzled
Death on the mouth that ate the gas.

Sharp in my second death I marked the hills, harvest
Of hemlock and the blades, rust
My blood upon the tempered dead, forcing
My second struggling from the grass.

And power was contagious in my birth, second
Rise of the skeleton and
Rerobing of the naked ghost. Manhood
Spat up from the resuffered pain.

I dreamed my genesis in sweat of death, fallen
Twice in the feeding sea, grown
Stale of Adam's brine until, vision
Of new man strength, I seek the sun.

I

Half of the fellow father as he doubles
His sea-sucked Adam in the hollow hulk,
Half of the fellow mother as she dabbles
To-morrow's diver in her horny milk,
Bisected shadows on the thunder's bone
Bolt for the salt unborn.

The fellow half was frozen as it bubbled
Corrosive spring out of the iceberg's crop,
The fellow seed and shadow as it babbled
The swing of milk was tufted in the pap,
For half of love was planted in the lost,
And the unplanted ghost.

The broken halves are fellowed in a cripple,
The crutch that marrow taps upon their sleep,
Limp in the street of sea, among the rabble
Of tide-tongued heads and bladders in the deep,
And stake the sleepers in the savage grave
That the vampire laugh.

The patchwork halves were cloven as they scudded
The wild pigs' wood, and slime upon the trees,
Sucking the dark, kissed on the cyanide,
And loosed the braiding adders from their hairs;
Rotating halves are horning as they drill
The arterial angel.

What colour is glory? death's feather? tremble
The halves that pierce the pin's point in the air,
And prick the thumb-stained heaven through the thimble.
The ghost is dumb that stammered in the straw,
The ghost that hatched his havoc as he flew
Blinds their cloud-tracking eye.

II

My world is pyramid. The padded mummer
Weeps on the desert ochre and the salt
Incising summer.
My Egypt's armour buckling in its sheet,
I scrape through resin to a starry bone
And a blood parhelion.

My world is cypress, and an English valley.
I piece my flesh that rattled on the yards
Red in an Austrian volley.
I hear, through dead men's drums, the riddled lads,
Strewing their bowels from a hill of bones,
Cry Eloi to the guns.

My grave is watered by the crossing Jordan.
The Arctic scut, and basin of the South,
Drip on my dead house garden.
Who seek me landward, marking in my mouth
The straws of Asia, lose me as I turn
Through the Atlantic corn.

The fellow halves that, cloven as they swivel
On casting tides, are tangled in the shells,
Bearding the unborn devil,
Bleed from my burning fork and smell my heels.
The tongues of heaven gossip as I glide
Binding my angel's hood.

Who blows death's feather? What glory is colour?
I blow the stammel feather in the vein.
The loin is glory in a working pallor.
My clay unsuckled and my salt unborn,
The secret child, I shift about the sea
Dry in the half-tracked thigh.

I

All all and all the dry worlds lever,
Stage of the ice, the solid ocean,
All from the oil, the pound of lava.
City of spring, the governed flower,
Turns in the earth that turns the ashen
Towns around on a wheel of fire.

How now my flesh, my naked fellow,
Dug of the sea, the glanded morrow,
Worm in the scalp, the staked and fallow.
All all and all, the corpse's lover,
Skinny as sin, the foaming marrow,
All of the flesh, the dry worlds lever.

II

Fear not the working world, my mortal,
Fear not the flat, synthetic blood,
Nor the heart in the ribbing metal.
Fear not the tread, the seeded milling,
The trigger and scythe, the bridal blade,
Nor the flint in the lover's mauling.

Man of my flesh, the jawbone riven,
Know now the flesh's lock and vice,
And the cage for the scythe-eyed raven.
Know, O my bone, the jointed lever,
Fear not the screws that turn the voice,
And the face to the driven lover.

III

All all and all the dry worlds couple,
Ghost with her ghost, contagious man
With the womb of his shapeless people.
All that shapes from the caul and suckle,
Stroke of mechanical flesh on mine,
Square in these worlds the mortal circle.

Flower, flower the people's fusion,
O light in zenith, the coupled bud,
And the flame in the flesh's vision.
Out of the sea, the drive of oil,
Socket and grave, the brassy blood,
Flower, flower, all all and all.

I

I, in my intricate image, stride on two levels,
Forged in man's minerals, the brassy orator
Laying my ghost in metal,
The scales of this twin world tread on the double,
My half ghost in armour hold hard in death's corridor,
To my man-iron sidle.

Beginning with doom in the bulb, the spring unravels,
Bright as her spinning-wheels, the colic season
Worked on a world of petals;
She threads off the sap and needles, blood and bubble
Casts to the pine roots, raising man like a mountain
Out of the naked entrail.

Beginning with doom in the ghost, and the springing marvels,
Image of images, my metal phantom
Forcing forth through the harebell,
My man of leaves and the bronze root, mortal, unmortal,
I, in my fusion of rose and male motion,
Create this twin miracle.

This is the fortune of manhood: the natural peril,
A steeplejack tower, bonerailed and masterless,
No death more natural;
Thus the shadowless man or ox, and the pictured devil,
In seizure of silence commit the dead nuisance:
The natural parallel.

My images stalk the trees and the slant sap's tunnel,
No tread more perilous, the green steps and spire
Mount on man's footfall,
I with the wooden insect in the tree of nettles,
In the glass bed of grapes with snail and flower,
Hearing the weather fall.

Intricate manhood of ending, the invalid rivals,
Voyaging clockwise off the symboled harbour,
Finding the water final,
On the consumptives' terrace taking their two farewells,
Sail on the level, the departing adventure,
To the sea-blown arrival.

II

They climb the country pinnacle,
Twelve winds encounter by the white host at pasture,
Corner the mounted meadows in the hill corral;
They see the squirrel stumble,
The haring snail go giddily round the flower,
A quarrel of weathers and trees in the windy spiral.

As they dive, the dust settles,
The cadaverous gravels, falls thick and steadily,
The highroad of water where the seabear and mackerel

Turn the long sea arterial
Turning a petrol face blind to the enemy
Turning the riderless dead by the channel wall.

(Death instrumental,
Splitting the long eye open, and the spiral turnkey,
Your corkscrew grave centred in navel and nipple,
The neck of the nostril,
Under the mask and the ether, they making bloody
The tray of knives, the antiseptic funeral;

Bring out the black patrol,
Your monstrous officers and the decaying army,
The sexton sentinel, garrisoned under thistles,
A cock-on-a-dunghill
Crowing to Lazarus the morning is vanity,
Dust be your saviour under the conjured soil.)

As they drown, the chime travels,
Sweetly the diver's bell in the steeple of spindrift
Rings out the Dead Sea scale;
And, clapped in water till the triton dangles,
Strung by the flaxen whale-weed, from the hangman's raft,
Hear they the salt glass breakers and the tongues of burial.

(Turn the sea-spindle lateral,
The grooved land rotating, that the stylus of lightning

Dazzle this face of voices on the moon-turned table,
Let the wax disk babble
Shames and the damp dishonours, the relic scraping.
These are your years' recorders. The circular world stands
    still.)

III

They suffer the undead water where the turtle nibbles,
Come unto sea-stuck towers, at the fibre scaling,
The flight of the carnal skull
And the cell-stepped thimble;
Suffer, my topsy-turvies, that a double angel
Sprout from the stony lockers like a tree on Aran.

Be by your one ghost pierced, his pointed ferrule,
Brass and the bodiless image, on a stick of folly
Star-set at Jacob's angle,
Smoke hill and hophead's valley,
And the five-fathomed Hamlet on his father's coral,
Thrusting the tom-thumb vision up the iron mile.

Suffer the slash of vision by the fin-green stubble,
Be by the ships' sea broken at the manstring anchored
The stoved bones' voyage downward
In the shipwreck of muscle;

Give over, lovers, locking, and the seawax struggle,
Love like a mist or fire through the bed of eels.

And in the pincers of the boiling circle,
The sea and instrument, nicked in the locks of time,
My great blood's iron single
In the pouring town,
I, in a wind on fire, from green Adam's cradle,
No man more magical, clawed out the crocodile.

Man was the scales, the death birds on enamel,
Tail, Nile, and snout, a saddler of the rushes,
Time in the hourless houses
Shaking the sea-hatched skull,
And, as for oils and ointments on the flying grail,
All-hollowed man wept for his white apparel.

Man was Cadaver's masker, the harnessing mantle,
Windily master of man was the rotten fathom,
My ghost in his metal neptune
Forged in man's mineral.
This was the god of beginning in the intricate seawhirl,
And my images roared and rose on heaven's hill.

This bread I break was once the oat,
This wine upon a foreign tree
Plunged in its fruit;
Man in the day or wind at night
Laid the crops low, broke the grape's joy.

Once in this wine the summer blood
Knocked in the flesh that decked the vine,
Once in this bread
The oat was merry in the wind;
Man broke the sun, pulled the wind down.

This flesh you break, this blood you let
Make desolation in the vein,
Were oat and grape
Born of the sensual root and sap;
My wine you drink, my bread you snap.

Incarnate devil in a talking snake,
The central plains of Asia in his garden,
In shaping-time the circle stung awake,
In shapes of sin forked out the bearded apple,
And God walked there who was a fiddling warden
And played down pardon from the heavens' hill.

When we were strangers to the guided seas,
A handmade moon half holy in a cloud,
The wisemen tell me that the garden gods
Twined good and evil on an eastern tree;
And when the moon rose windily it was
Black as the beast and paler than the cross.

We in our Eden knew the secret guardian
In sacred waters that no frost could harden,
And in the mighty mornings of the earth;
Hell in a horn of sulphur and the cloven myth,
All heaven in a midnight of the sun,
A serpent fiddled in the shaping-time.

To-day, this insect, and the world I breathe,
Now that my symbols have outelbowed space,
Time at the city spectacles, and half
The dear, daft time I take to nudge the sentence,
In trust and tale have I divided sense,
Slapped down the guillotine, the blood-red double
Of head and tail made witnesses to this
Murder of Eden and green genesis.

The insect certain is the plague of fables.

This story's monster has a serpent caul,
Blind in the coil scrams round the blazing outline,
Measures his own length on the garden wall
And breaks his shell in the last shocked beginning;
A crocodile before the chrysalis,
Before the fall from love the flying heartbone,
Winged like a sabbath ass this children's piece
Uncredited blows Jericho on Eden.

The insect fable is the certain promise.

Death: death of Hamlet and the nightmare madmen,
An air-drawn windmill on a wooden horse,
John's beast, Job's patience, and the fibs of vision,
Greek in the Irish sea the ageless voice:
'Adam I love, my madmen's love is endless,
No tell-tale lover has an end more certain,
All legends' sweethearts on a tree of stories,
My cross of tales behind the fabulous curtain.'

The seed-at-zero shall not storm
That town of ghosts, the trodden womb
With her rampart to his tapping,
No god-in-hero tumble down
Like a tower on the town
Dumbly and divinely stumbling
Over the manwaging line.

The seed-at-zero shall not storm
That town of ghosts, the manwaged womb
With her rampart to his tapping,
No god-in-hero tumble down
Like a tower on the town
Dumbly and divinely leaping
Over the warbearing line.

Through the rampart of the sky
Shall the star-flanked seed be riddled,
Manna for the rumbling ground,
Quickening for the riddled sea;
Settled on a virgin stronghold
He shall grapple with the guard
And the keeper of the key.

Through the rampart of the sky
Shall the star-flanked seed be riddled,
Manna for the guarded ground,
Quickening for the virgin sea;
Settling on a riddled stronghold
He shall grapple with the guard
And the loser of the key.

May a humble village labour
And a continent deny?
A hemisphere may scold him
And a green inch be his bearer;
Let the hero seed find harbour,
Seaports by a drunken shore
Have their thirsty sailors hide him.

May a humble planet labour
And a continent deny?
A village green may scold him
And a high sphere be his bearer;
Let the hero seed find harbour,
Seaports by a thirsty shore
Have their drunken sailors hide him.

Man-in-seed, in seed-at-zero,
From the foreign fields of space,
Shall not thunder on the town
With a star-flanked garrison,
Nor the cannons of his kingdom
Shall the hero-in-tomorrow
Range on the sky-scraping place.

Man-in-seed, in seed-at-zero,
From the star-flanked fields of space,
Thunders on the foreign town
With a sand-bagged garrison,
Nor the cannons of his kingdom
Shall the hero-in-to-morrow
Range from the grave-groping place.

Shall gods be said to thump the clouds
When clouds are cursed by thunder,
Be said to weep when weather howls?
Shall rainbows be their tunics' colour?

When it is rain where are the gods?
Shall it be said they sprinkle water
From garden cans, or free the floods?

Shall it be said that, venuswise,
An old god's dugs are pressed and pricked,
The wet night scolds me like a nurse?

It shall be said that gods are stone.
Shall a dropped stone drum on the ground,
Flung gravel chime? Let the stones speak
With tongues that talk all tongues.

Here in this spring, stars float along the void;
Here in this ornamental winter
Down pelts the naked weather;
This summer buries a spring bird.

Symbols are selected from the years'
Slow rounding of four seasons' coasts,
In autumn teach three seasons' fires
And four birds' notes.

I should tell summer from the trees, the worms
Tell, if at all, the winter's storms
Or the funeral of the sun;
I should learn spring by the cuckooing,
And the slug should teach me destruction.

A worm tells summer better than the clock,
The slug's a living calendar of days;
What shall it tell me if a timeless insect
Says the world wears away?

Do you not father me, nor the erected arm
For my tall tower's sake cast in her stone?
Do you not mother me, nor, as I am,
The lovers' house, lie suffering my stain?
Do you not sister me, nor the erected crime
For my tall turrets carry as your sin?
Do you not brother me, nor, as you climb,
Adore my windows for their summer scene?

Am I not father, too, and the ascending boy,
The boy of woman and the wanton starer
Marking the flesh and summer in the bay?
Am I not sister, too, who is my saviour?
Am I not all of you by the directed sea
Where bird and shell are babbling in my tower?
Am I not you who front the tidy shore,
Nor roof of sand, nor yet the towering tiler?

You are all these, said she who gave me the long suck,
All these, he said who sacked the children's town,
Up rose the Abraham-man, mad for my sake,
They said, who hacked and humoured, they were mine.
I am, the tower told, felled by a timeless stroke,
Who razed my wooden folly stands aghast,
For man-begetters in the dry-as-paste,
The ringed-sea ghost, rise grimly from the wrack.

Do you not father me on the destroying sand?
You are your sisters' sire, said seaweedy,
The salt sucked dam and darlings of the land
Who play the proper gentleman and lady.
Shall I still be love's house on the widdershin earth,
Woe to the windy masons at my shelter?
Love's house, they answer, and the tower death
Lie all unknowing of the grave sin-eater.

Out of the sighs a little comes,
But not of grief, for I have knocked down that
Before the agony; the spirit grows,
Forgets, and cries;
A little comes, is tasted and found good;
All could not disappoint;
There must, be praised, some certainty,
If not of loving well, then not,
And that is true after perpetual defeat.

After such fighting as the weakest know,
There's more than dying;
Lose the great pains or stuff the wound,
He'll ache too long
Through no regret of leaving woman waiting
For her soldier stained with spilt words
That spill such acrid blood.

Were that enough, enough to ease the pain,
Feeling regret when this is wasted
That made me happy in the sun,
How much was happy while it lasted,
Were vagueness enough and the sweet lies plenty,
The hollow words could bear all suffering
And cure me of ills.

Were that enough, bone, blood, and sinew,
The twisted brain, the fair-formed loin,
Groping for matter under the dog's plate,
Man should be cured of distemper.
For all there is to give I offer:
Crumbs, barn, and halter.

Hold hard, these ancient minutes in the cuckoo's month,
Under the lank, fourth folly on Glamorgan's hill,
As the green blooms ride upward, to the drive of time;
Time, in a folly's rider, like a county man
Over the vault of ridings with his hound at heel,
Drives forth my men, my children, from the hanging south.

Country, your sport is summer, and December's pools
By crane and water-tower by the seedy trees
Lie this fifth month unskated, and the birds have flown;
Hold hard, my country children in the world of tales,
The greenwood dying as the deer fall in their tracks,
This first and steepled season, to the summer's game.

And now the horns of England, in the sound of shape,
Summon your snowy horsemen, and the four-stringed hill,
Over the sea-gut loudening, sets a rock alive;
Hurdles and guns and railings, as the boulders heave,
Crack like a spring in a vice, bone breaking April,
Spill the lank folly's hunter and the hard-held hope.

Down fall four padding weathers on the scarlet lands,
Stalking my children's faces with a tail of blood,
Time, in a rider rising, from the harnessed valley;
Hold hard, my county darlings, for a hawk descends,
Golden Glamorgan straightens, to the falling birds.
Your sport is summer as the spring runs angrily.

Was there a time when dancers with their fiddles
In children's circuses could stay their troubles?
There was a time they could cry over books,
But time has set its maggot on their track.
Under the arc of the sky they are unsafe.
What's never known is safest in this life.
Under the skysigns they who have no arms
Have cleanest hands, and, as the heartless ghost
Alone's unhurt, so the blind man sees best.

Now
Say nay,
Man dry man,
Dry lover mine
The deadrock base and blow the flowered anchor,
Should he, for centre sake, hop in the dust,
Forsake, the fool, the hardiness of anger.

Now
Say nay,
Sir no say,
Death to the yes,
The yes to death, the yesman and the answer,
Should he who split his children with a cure
Have brotherless his sister on the handsaw.

Now
Say nay,
No say sir
Yea the dead stir,
And this, nor this, is shade, the landed crow,
He lying low with ruin in his ear,
The cockerel's tide upcasting from the fire.

Now
Say nay,
So star fall,
So the ball fail,
So solve the mystic sun, the wife of light,
The sun that leaps on petals through a nought,
The come-a-cropper rider of the flower.

Now
Say nay
A fig for
The seal of fire,
Death hairy-heeled, and the tapped ghost in wood,
We make me mystic as the arm of air,
The two-a-vein, the foreskin, and the cloud.

Why east wind chills and south wind cools
Shall not be known till windwell dries
And west's no longer drowned
In winds that bring the fruit and rind
Of many a hundred falls;
Why silk is soft and the stone wounds
The child shall question all his days,
Why night-time rain and the breast's blood
Both quench his thirst he'll have a black reply.

When cometh Jack Frost? the children ask.
Shall they clasp a comet in their fists?
Not till, from high and low, their dust
Sprinkles in children's eyes a long-last sleep
And dusk is crowded with the children's ghosts,
Shall a white answer echo from the rooftops.

All things are known: the stars' advice
Calls some content to travel with the winds,
Though what the stars ask as they round
Time upon time the towers of the skies
Is heard but little till the stars go out.
I hear content, and 'Be content'
Ring like a handbell through the corridors,
And 'Know no answer,' and I know
No answer to the children's cry
Of echo's answer and the man of frost
And ghostly comets over the raised fists.

A grief ago,
She who was who I hold, the fats and flower,
Or, water-lammed, from the scythe-sided thorn,
Hell wind and sea,
A stem cementing, wrestled up the tower,
Rose maid and male,
Or, masted venus, through the paddler's bowl
Sailed up the sun;

Who is my grief,
A chrysalis unwrinkling on the iron,
Wrenched by my fingerman, the leaden bud
Shot through the leaf,
Was who was folded on the rod the aaron
Rose cast to plague,
The horn and ball of water on the frog
Housed in the side.

And she who lies,
Like exodus a chapter from the garden,
Brand of the lily's anger on her ring,
Tugged through the days
Her ropes of heritage, the wars of pardon,
On field and sand
The twelve triangles of the cherub wind
Engraving going.

Who then is she,
She holding me? The people's sea drives on her,
Drives out the father from the caesared camp;
The dens of shape
Shape all her whelps with the long voice of water,
That she I have,
The country-handed grave boxed into love,
Rise before dark.

The night is near,
A nitric shape that leaps her, time and acid;
I tell her this: before the suncock cast
Her bone to fire,
Let her inhale her dead, through seed and solid
Draw in their seas,
So cross her hand with their grave gipsy eyes,
And close her fist.

How soon the servant sun,
(Sir morrow mark),
Can time unriddle, and the cupboard stone,
(Fog has a bone
He'll trumpet into meat),
Unshelve that all my gristles have a gown
And the naked egg stand straight,

Sir morrow at his sponge,
(The wound records),
The nurse of giants by the cut sea basin,
(Fog by his spring
Soaks up the sewing tides),
Tells you and you, my masters, as his strange
Man morrow blows through food.

All nerves to serve the sun,
The rite of light,
A claw I question from the mouse's bone,
The long-tailed stone
Trap I with coil and sheet,
Let the soil squeal I am the biting man
And the velvet dead inch out.

How soon my level, lord,
(Sir morrow stamps
Two heels of water on the floor of seed),
Shall raise a lamp
Or spirit up a cloud,
Erect a walking centre in the shroud,
Invisible on the stump

A leg as long as trees,
This inward sir,
Mister and master, darkness for his eyes,
The womb-eyed, cries,
And all sweet hell, deaf as an hour's ear,
Blasts back the trumpet voice.

Ears in the turrets hear
Hands grumble on the door,
Eyes in the gables see
The fingers at the locks.
Shall I unbolt or stay
Alone till the day I die
Unseen by stranger-eyes
In this white house?
Hands, hold you poison or grapes?

Beyond this island bound
By a thin sea of flesh
And a bone coast,
The land lies out of sound
And the hills out of mind.
No birds or flying fish
Disturbs this island's rest.

Ears in this island hear
The wind pass like a fire,
Eyes in this island see
Ships anchor off the bay.
Shall I run to the ships
With the wind in my hair,
Or stay till the day I die
And welcome no sailor?
Ships, hold you poison or grapes?

Hands grumble on the door,
Ships anchor off the bay,
Rain beats the sand and slates.
Shall I let in the stranger,
Shall I welcome the sailor,
Or stay till the day I die?

Hands of the stranger and holds of the ships,
Hold you poison or grapes?

Foster the light nor veil the manshaped moon,
Nor weather winds that blow not down the bone,
But strip the twelve-winded marrow from his circle;
Master the night nor serve the snowman's brain
That shapes each bushy item of the air
Into a polestar pointed on an icicle.

Murmur of spring nor crush the cockerel's eggs,
Nor hammer back a season in the figs,
But graft these four-fruited ridings on your country;
Farmer in time of frost the burning leagues,
By red-eyed orchards sow the seeds of snow,
In your young years the vegetable century.

And father all nor fail the fly-lord's acre,
Nor sprout on owl-seed like a goblin-sucker,
But rail with your wizard's ribs the heart-shaped planet;
Of mortal voices to the ninnies' choir,
High lord esquire, speak up the singing cloud,
And pluck a mandrake music from the marrowroot.

Roll unmanly over this turning tuft,
O ring of seas, nor sorrow as I shift
From all my mortal lovers with a starboard smile;
Nor when my love lies in the cross-boned drift
Naked among the bow-and-arrow birds
Shall you turn cockwise on a tufted axle.

Who gave these seas their colour in a shape,
Shaped my clayfellow, and the heaven's ark
In time at flood filled with his coloured doubles;
O who is glory in the shapeless maps,
Now make the world of me as I have made
A merry manshape of your walking circle.

The hand that signed the paper felled a city;
Five sovereign fingers taxed the breath,
Doubled the globe of dead and halved a country;
These five kings did a king to death.

The mighty hand leads to a sloping shoulder,
The finger joints are cramped with chalk;
A goose's quill has put an end to murder
That put an end to talk.

The hand that signed the treaty bred a fever,
And famine grew, and locusts came;
Great is the hand that holds dominion over
Man by a scribbled name.

The five kings count the dead but do not soften
The crusted wound nor stroke the brow;
A hand rules pity as a hand rules heaven;
Hands have no tears to flow.

Should lanterns shine, the holy face,
Caught in an octagon of unaccustomed light,
Would wither up, and any boy of love
Look twice before he fell from grace.
The features in their private dark
Are formed of flesh, but let the false day come
And from her lips the faded pigments fall,
The mummy cloths expose an ancient breast.

I have been told to reason by the heart,
But heart, like head, leads helplessly;
I have been told to reason by the pulse,
And, when it quickens, alter the actions' pace
Till field and roof lie level and the same
So fast I move defying time, the quiet gentleman
Whose beard wags in Egyptian wind.

I have heard many years of telling,
And many years should see some change.

The ball I threw while playing in the park
Has not yet reached the ground.

I have longed to move away
From the hissing of the spent lie
And the old terrors' continual cry
Growing more terrible as the day
Goes over the hill into the deep sea;
I have longed to move away
From the repetition of salutes,
From there are ghosts in the air
And ghostly echoes on paper,
And the thunder of calls and notes.

I have longed to move away but am afraid;
Some life, yet unspent, might explode
Out of the old lie burning on the ground,
And, crackling into the air, leave me half-blind.
Neither by night's ancient fear,
The parting of hat from hair,
Pursed lips at the receiver,
Shall I fall to death's feather.
By these I would not care to die,
Half convention and half lie.

'Find meat on bones that soon have none,
And drink in the two milked crags,
The merriest marrow and the dregs
Before the ladies' breasts are hags
And the limbs are torn.
Disturb no winding-sheets, my son,
But when the ladies are cold as stone
Then hang a ram rose over the rags.

'Rebel against the binding moon
And the parliament of sky,
The kingcrafts of the wicked sea,
Autocracy of night and day,
Dictatorship of sun.
Rebel against the flesh and bone,
The word of the blood, the wily skin,
And the maggot no man can slay.'

'The thirst is quenched, the hunger gone,
And my heart is cracked across;
My face is haggard in the glass,
My lips are withered with a kiss,
My breasts are thin.
A merry girl took me for man,
I laid her down and told her sin,
And put beside her a ram rose.

'The maggot that no man can kill
And the man no rope can hang
Rebel against my father's dream
That out of a bower of red swine
Howls the foul fiend to heel.
I cannot murder, like a fool,
Season and sunshine, grace and girl,
Nor can I smother the sweet waking.'

Black night still ministers the moon,
And the sky lays down her laws,
The sea speaks in a kingly voice,
Light and dark are no enemies
But one companion.
'War on the spider and the wren!
War on the destiny of man!
Doom on the sun!'
Before death takes you, O take back this.

Grief thief of time crawls off,
The moon-drawn grave, with the seafaring years,
The knave of pain steals off
The sea-halved faith that blew time to his knees,
The old forget the cries,
Lean time on tide and times the wind stood rough,
Call back the castaways
Riding the sea light on a sunken path,
The old forget the grief,
Hack of the cough, the hanging albatross,
Cast back the bone of youth
And salt-eyed stumble bedward where she lies
Who tossed the high tide in a time of stories
And timelessly lies loving with the thief.

Now Jack my fathers let the time-faced crook,
Death flashing from his sleeve,
With swag of bubbles in a seedy sack
Sneak down the stallion grave,
Bull's-eye the outlaw through a eunuch crack
And free the twin-boxed grief,
No silver whistles chase him down the weeks'
Dayed peaks to day to death,
These stolen bubbles have the bites of snakes
And the undead eye-teeth,
No third eye probe into a rainbow's sex
That bridged the human halves,
All shall remain and on the graveward gulf
Shape with my fathers' thieves.

[76]

And death shall have no dominion.
Dead men naked they shall be one
With the man in the wind and the west moon;
When their bones are picked clean and the clean bones gone,
They shall have stars at elbow and foot;
Though they go mad they shall be sane,
Though they sink through the sea they shall rise again;
Though lovers be lost love shall not;
And death shall have no dominion.

And death shall have no dominion.
Under the windings of the sea
They lying long shall not die windily;
Twisting on racks when sinews give way,
Strapped to a wheel, yet they shall not break;
Faith in their hands shall snap in two,
And the unicorn evils run them through;
Split all ends up they shan't crack;
And death shall have no dominion.

And death shall have no dominion.
No more may gulls cry at their ears
Or waves break loud on the seashores;
Where blew a flower may a flower no more
Lift its head to the blows of the rain;
Though they be mad and dead as nails,
Heads of the characters hammer through daisies;
Break in the sun till the sun breaks down,
And death shall have no dominion.

Then was my neophyte,
Child in white blood bent on its knees
Under the bell of rocks,
Ducked in the twelve, disciple seas
The winder of the water-clocks
Calls a green day and night.
My sea hermaphrodite,
Snail of man in His ship of fires
That burn the bitten decks,
Knew all His horrible desires
The climber of the water sex
Calls the green rock of light.

Who in these labyrinths,
This tidethread and the lane of scales,
Twine in a moon-blown shell,
Escapes to the flat cities' sails
Furled on the fishes' house and hell,
Nor falls to His green myths?
Stretch the salt photographs,
The landscape grief, love in His oils
Mirror from man to whale
That the green child see like a grail
Through veil and fin and fire and coil
Time on the canvas paths.

He films my vanity.
Shot in the wind, by tilted arcs,
Over the water come
Children from homes and children's parks
Who speak on a finger and thumb,
And the masked, headless boy.
His reels and mystery
The winder of the clockwise scene
Wound like a ball of lakes
Then threw on that tide-hoisted screen
Love's image till my heartbone breaks
By a dramatic sea.

Who kills my history?
The year-hedged row is lame with flint,
Blunt scythe and water blade.
'Who could snap off the shapeless print
From your to-morrow-treading shade
With oracle for eye?'
Time kills me terribly.
'Time shall not murder you,' He said,
'Nor the green nought be hurt;
Who could hack out your unsucked heart,
O green and unborn and undead?'
I saw time murder me.

I

Altarwise by owl-light in the half-way house
The gentleman lay graveward with his furies;
Abaddon in the hangnail cracked from Adam,
And, from his fork, a dog among the fairies,
The atlas-eater with a jaw for news,
Bit out the mandrake with to-morrow's scream.
Then, penny-eyed, that gentleman of wounds,
Old cock from nowheres and the heaven's egg,
With bones unbuttoned to the half-way winds,
Hatched from the windy salvage on one leg,
Scraped at my cradle in a walking word
That night of time under the Christward shelter:
I am the long world's gentleman, he said,
And share my bed with Capricorn and Cancer.

II

Death is all metaphors, shape in one history;
The child that sucketh long is shooting up,
The planet-ducted pelican of circles
Weans on an artery the gender's strip;
Child of the short spark in a shapeless country
Soon sets alight a long stick from the cradle;
The horizontal cross-bones of Abaddon,
You by the cavern over the black stairs,
Rung bone and blade, the verticals of Adam,
And, manned by midnight, Jacob to the stars.

Hairs of your head, then said the hollow agent,
Are but the roots of nettles and of feathers
Over these groundworks thrusting through a pavement
And hemlock-headed in the wood of weathers.

III

First there was the lamb on knocking knees
And three dead seasons on a climbing grave
That Adam's wether in the flock of horns,
Butt of the tree-tailed worm that mounted Eve,
Horned down with skullfoot and the skull of toes
On thunderous pavements in the garden time;
Rip of the vaults, I took my marrow-ladle
Out of the wrinkled undertaker's van,
And, Rip Van Winkle from a timeless cradle,
Dipped me breast-deep in the descended bone;
The black ram, shuffling of the year, old winter,
Alone alive among his mutton fold,
We rung our weathering changes on the ladder,
Said the antipodes, and twice spring chimed.

IV

What is the metre of the dictionary?
The size of genesis? the short spark's gender?
Shade without shape? the shape of Pharaoh's echo?
(My shape of age nagging the wounded whisper).

Which sixth of wind blew out the burning gentry?
(Questions are hunchbacks to the poker marrow).
What of a bamboo man among your acres?
Corset the boneyards for a crooked boy?
Button your bodice on a hump of splinters,
My camel's eyes will needle through the shrowd.
Love's reflection of the mushroom features,
Stills snapped by night in the bread-sided field,
Once close-up smiling in the wall of pictures,
Arc-lamped thrown back upon the cutting flood.

v

And from the windy West came two-gunned Gabriel,
From Jesu's sleeve trumped up the king of spots,
The sheath-decked jacks, queen with a shuffled heart;
Said the fake gentleman in suit of spades,
Black-tongued and tipsy from salvation's bottle.
Rose my Byzantine Adam in the night.
For loss of blood I fell on Ishmael's plain,
Under the milky mushrooms slew my hunger,
A climbing sea from Asia had me down
And Jonah's Moby snatched me by the hair,
Cross-stroked salt Adam to the frozen angel
Pin-legged on pole-hills with a black medusa
By waste seas where the white bear quoted Virgil
And sirens singing from our lady's sea-straw.

VI

Cartoon of slashes on the tide-traced crater,
He in a book of water tallow-eyed
By lava's light split through the oyster vowels
And burned sea silence on a wick of words.
Pluck, cock, my sea eye, said medusa's scripture,
Lop, love, my fork tongue, said the pin-hilled nettle;
And love plucked out the stinging siren's eye,
Old cock from nowheres lopped the minstrel tongue
Till tallow I blew from the wax's tower
The fats of midnight when the salt was singing;
Adam, time's joker, on a witch of cardboard
Spelt out the seven seas, an evil index,
The bagpipe-breasted ladies in the deadweed
Blew out the blood gauze through the wound of manwax.

VII

Now stamp the Lord's Prayer on a grain of rice,
A Bible-leaved of all the written woods
Strip to this tree: a rocking alphabet,
Genesis in the root, the scarecrow word,
And one light's language in the book of trees.
Doom on deniers at the wind-turned statement.
Time's tune my ladies with the teats of music,
The scaled sea-sawers, fix in a naked sponge
Who sucks the bell-voiced Adam out of magic,
Time, milk, and magic, from the world beginning.

[83]

Time is the tune my ladies lend their heartbreak,
From bald pavilions and the house of bread
Time tracks the sound of shape on man and cloud,
On rose and icicle the ringing handprint.

VIII

This was the crucifixion on the mountain,
Time's nerve in vinegar, the gallow grave
As tarred with blood as the bright thorns I wept;
The world's my wound, God's Mary in her grief,
Bent like three trees and bird-papped through her shift,
With pins for teardrops is the long wound's woman.
This was the sky, Jack Christ, each minstrel angle
Drove in the heaven-driven of the nails
Till the three-coloured rainbow from my nipples
From pole to pole leapt round the snail-waked world.
I by the tree of thieves, all glory's sawbones,
Unsex the skeleton this mountain minute,
And by this blowclock witness of the sun
Suffer the heaven's children through my heartbeat.

IX

From the oracular archives and the parchment,
Prophets and fibre kings in oil and letter,
The lamped calligrapher, the queen in splints,
Buckle to lint and cloth their natron footsteps,
Draw on the glove of prints, dead Cairo's henna
Pour like a halo on the caps and serpents.

This was the resurrection in the desert,
Death from a bandage, rants the mask of scholars
Gold on such features, and the linen spirit
Weds my long gentleman to dusts and furies;
With priest and pharaoh bed my gentle wound,
World in the sand, on the triangle landscape,
With stones of odyssey for ash and garland
And rivers of the dead around my neck.

X

Let the tale's sailor from a Christian voyage
Atlaswise hold half-way off the dummy bay
Time's ship-racked gospel on the globe I balance:
So shall winged harbours through the rockbirds' eyes
Spot the blown word, and on the seas I image
December's thorn screwed in a brow of holly.
Let the first Peter from a rainbow's quayrail
Ask the tall fish swept from the bible east,
What rhubarb man peeled in her foam-blue channel
Has sown a flying garden round that sea-ghost?
Green as beginning, let the garden diving
Soar, with its two bark towers, to that Day
When the worm builds with the gold straws of venom
My nest of mercies in the rude, red tree.

Because the pleasure-bird whistles after the hot wires,
Shall the blind horse sing sweeter?
Convenient bird and beast lie lodged to suffer
The supper and knives of a mood.
In the sniffed and poured snow on the tip of the tongue of the
     year
That clouts the spittle like bubbles with broken rooms,
An enamoured man alone by the twigs of his eyes, two fires,
Camped in the drug-white shower of nerves and food,
Savours the lick of the times through a deadly wood of hair
In a wind that plucked a goose,
Nor ever, as the wild tongue breaks its tombs,
Rounds to look at the red, wagged root.
Because there stands, one story out of the bum city,
That frozen wife whose juices drift like a fixed sea
Secretly in statuary,
Shall I, struck on the hot and rocking street,
Not spin to stare at an old year
Toppling and burning in the muddle of towers and galleries
Like the mauled pictures of boys?
The salt person and blasted place
I furnish with the meat of a fable;
If the dead starve, their stomachs turn to tumble
An upright man in the antipodes
Or spray-based and rock-chested sea:
Over the past table I repeat this present grace.

I make this in a warring absence when
Each ancient, stone-necked minute of love's season
Harbours my anchored tongue, slips the quaystone,
When, praise is blessed, her pride in mast and fountain
Sailed and set dazzling by the handshaped ocean,
In that proud sailing tree with branches driven
Through the last vault and vegetable groyne,
And this weak house to marrow-columned heaven,

Is corner-cast, breath's rag, scrawled weed, a vain
And opium head, crow stalk, puffed, cut, and blown,
Or like the tide-looped breastknot reefed again
Or rent ancestrally the roped sea-hymen,
And, pride is last, is like a child alone
By magnet winds to her blind mother drawn,
Bread and milk mansion in a toothless town.

She makes for me a nettle's innocence
And a silk pigeon's guilt in her proud absence,
In the molested rocks the shell of virgins,
The frank, closed pearl, the sea-girls' lineaments
Glint in the staved and siren-printed caverns,
Is maiden in the shameful oak, omens
Whalebed and bulldance, the gold bush of lions,
Proud as a sucked stone and huge as sandgrains.

These are her contraries: the beast who follows
With priest's grave foot and hand of five assassins
Her molten flight up cinder-nesting columns,
Calls the starved fire herd, is cast in ice,
Lost in a limp-treed and uneating silence,
Who scales a hailing hill in her cold flintsteps
Falls on a ring of summers and locked noons.

I make a weapon of an ass's skeleton
And walk the warring sands by the dead town,
Cudgel great air, wreck east, and topple sundown,
Storm her sped heart, hang with beheaded veins
Its wringing shell, and let her eyelids fasten.
Destruction, picked by birds, brays through the jaw-bone,
And, for that murder's sake, dark with contagion
Like an approaching wave I sprawl to ruin.

Ruin, the room of errors, one rood dropped
Down the stacked sea and water-pillared shade,
Weighed in rock shroud, is my proud pyramid;
Where, wound in emerald linen and sharp wind,
The hero's head lies scraped of every legend,
Comes love's anatomist with sun-gloved hand
Who picks the live heart on a diamond.

'His mother's womb had a tongue that lapped up mud,'
Cried the topless, inchtaped lips from hank and hood
In that bright anchorground where I lay linened,
'A lizard darting with black venom's thread
Doubled, to fork him back, through the lockjaw bed
And the breath-white, curtained mouth of seed.'
'See,' drummed the taut masks, 'how the dead ascend:
In the groin's endless coil a man is tangled.'

These once-blind eyes have breathed a wind of visions,
The cauldron's root through this once-rindless hand
Fumed like a tree, and tossed a burning bird;
With loud, torn tooth and tail and cobweb drum
The crumpled packs fled past this ghost in bloom,
And, mild as pardon from a cloud of pride,
The terrible world my brother bares his skin.

Now in the cloud's big breast lie quiet countries,
Delivered seas my love from her proud place
Walks with no wound, nor lightning in her face,
A calm wind blows that raised the trees like hair
Once where the soft snow's blood was turned to ice.
And though my love pulls the pale, nippled air,
Prides of to-morrow suckling in her eyes,
Yet this I make in a forgiving presence.

When all my five and country senses see,
The fingers will forget green thumbs and mark
How, through the halfmoon's vegetable eye,
Husk of young stars and handfull zodiac,
Love in the frost is pared and wintered by,
The whispering ears will watch love drummed away
Down breeze and shell to a discordant beach,
And, lashed to syllables, the lynx tongue cry
That her fond wounds are mended bitterly.
My nostrils see her breath burn like a bush.

My one and noble heart has witnesses
In all love's countries, that will grope awake;
And when blind sleep drops on the spying senses,
The heart is sensual, though five eyes break.

We lying by seasand, watching yellow
And the grave sea, mock who deride
Who follow the red rivers, hollow
Alcove of words out of cicada shade,
For in this yellow grave of sand and sea
A calling for colour calls with the wind
That's grave and gay as grave and sea
Sleeping on either hand.
The lunar silences, the silent tide
Lapping the still canals, the dry tide-master
Ribbed between desert and water storm,
Should cure our ills of the water
With a one-coloured calm;
The heavenly music over the sand
Sounds with the grains as they hurry
Hiding the golden mountains and mansions
Of the grave, gay, seaside land.
Bound by a sovereign strip, we lie,
Watch yellow, wish for wind to blow away
The strata of the shore and drown red rock;
But wishes breed not, neither
Can we fend off rock arrival,
Lie watching yellow until the golden weather
Breaks, O my heart's blood, like a heart and hill.

It is the sinners' dust-tongued bell claps me to churches
When, with his torch and hourglass, like a sulphur priest,
His beast heel cleft in a sandal,
Time marks a black aisle kindle from the brand of ashes,
Grief with dishevelled hands tear out the altar ghost
And a firewind kill the candle.

Over the choir minute I hear the hour chant:
Time's coral saint and the salt grief drown a foul sepulchre
And a whirlpool drives the prayerwheel;
Moonfall and sailing emperor, pale as their tide-print,
Hear by death's accident the clocked and dashed-down spire
Strike the sea hour through bellmetal.

There is loud and dark directly under the dumb flame,
Storm, snow, and fountain in the weather of fireworks,
Cathedral calm in the pulled house;
Grief with drenched book and candle christens the cherub
    time
From the emerald, still bell; and from the pacing weather-
    cock
The voice of bird on coral prays.

Forever it is a white child in the dark-skinned summer
Out of the font of bone and plants at that stone tocsin
Scales the blue wall of spirits;
From blank and leaking winter sails the child in colour,
Shakes, in crabbed burial shawl, by sorcerer's insect woken,
Ding dong from the mute turrets.

I mean by time the cast and curfew rascal of our marriage,
At nightbreak born in the fat side, from an animal bed
In a holy room in a wave;
And all love's sinners in sweet cloth kneel to a hyleg image,
Nutmeg, civet, and sea-parsley serve the plagued groom and
        bride
Who have brought forth the urchin grief.

O make me a mask and a wall to shut from your spies
Of the sharp, enamelled eyes and the spectacled claws
Rape and rebellion in the nurseries of my face,
Gag of a dumbstruck tree to block from bare enemies
The bayonet tongue in this undefended prayerpiece,
The present mouth, and the sweetly blown trumpet of lies,
Shaped in old armour and oak the countenance of a dunce
To shield the glistening brain and blunt the examiners,
And a tear-stained widower grief drooped from the lashes
To veil belladonna and let the dry eyes perceive
Others betray the lamenting lies of their losses
By the curve of the nude mouth or the laugh up the sleeve.

The spire cranes. Its statue is an aviary.
From the stone nest it does not let the feathery
Carved birds blunt their striking throats on the salt gravel,
Pierce the spilt sky with diving wing in weed and heel
An inch in froth. Chimes cheat the prison spire, pelter
In time like outlaw rains on that priest, water,
Time for the swimmers' hands, music for silver lock
And mouth. Both note and plume plunge from the spire's
     hook.
Those craning birds are choice for you, songs that jump back
To the built voice, or fly with winter to the bells,
But do not travel down dumb wind like prodigals.

After the funeral, mule praises, brays,
Windshake of sailshaped ears, muffle-toed tap
Tap happily of one peg in the thick
Grave's foot, blinds down the lids, the teeth in black,
The spittled eyes, the salt ponds in the sleeves,
Morning smack of the spade that wakes up sleep,
Shakes a desolate boy who slits his throat
In the dark of the coffin and sheds dry leaves,
That breaks one bone to light with a judgment clout,
After the feast of tear-stuffed time and thistles
In a room with a stuffed fox and a stale fern,
I stand, for this memorial's sake, alone
In the snivelling hours with dead, humped Ann
Whose hooded, fountain heart once fell in puddles
Round the parched worlds of Wales and drowned each sun
(Though this for her is a monstrous image blindly
Magnified out of praise; her death was a still drop;
She would not have me sinking in the holy
Flood of her heart's fame; she would lie dumb and deep
And need no druid of her broken body).
But I, Ann's bard on a raised hearth, call all
The seas to service that her wood-tongued virtue
Babble like a bellbuoy over the hymning heads,
Bow down the walls of the ferned and foxy woods
That her love sing and swing through a brown chapel,
Bless her bent spirit with four, crossing birds.
Her flesh was meek as milk, but this skyward statue
With the wild breast and blessed and giant skull

Is carved from her in a room with a wet window
In a fiercely mourning house in a crooked year.
I know her scrubbed and sour humble hands
Lie with religion in their cramp, her threadbare
Whisper in a damp word, her wits drilled hollow,
Her fist of a face died clenched on a round pain;
And sculptured Ann is seventy years of stone.
These cloud-sopped, marble hands, this monumental
Argument of the hewn voice, gesture and psalm,
Storm me forever over her grave until
The stuffed lung of the fox twitch and cry Love
And the strutting fern lay seeds on the black sill.

Once it was the colour of saying
Soaked my table the uglier side of a hill
With a capsized field where a school sat still
And a black and white patch of girls grew playing;
The gentle seaslides of saying I must undo
That all the charmingly drowned arise to cockcrow and kill.
When I whistled with mitching boys through a reservoir park
Where at night we stoned the cold and cuckoo
Lovers in the dirt of their leafy beds,
The shade of their trees was a word of many shades
And a lamp of lightning for the poor in the dark;
Now my saying shall be my undoing,
And every stone I wind off like a reel.

Not from this anger, anticlimax after
Refusal struck her loin and the lame flower
Bent like a beast to lap the singular floods
In a land strapped by hunger
Shall she receive a bellyful of weeds
And bear those tendril hands I touch across
The agonized, two seas.
Behind my head a square of sky sags over
The circular smile tossed from lover to lover
And the golden ball spins out of the skies;
Not from this anger after
Refusal struck like a bell under water
Shall her smile breed that mouth, behind the mirror,
That burns along my eyes.

How shall my animal
Whose wizard shape I trace in the cavernous skull,
Vessel of abscesses and exultation's shell,
Endure burial under the spelling wall,
The invoked, shrouding veil at the cap of the face,
Who should be furious,
Drunk as a vineyard snail, flailed like an octopus,
Roaring, crawling, quarrel
With the outside weathers,
The natural circle of the discovered skies
Draw down to its weird eyes?

How shall it magnetize,
Towards the studded male in a bent, midnight blaze
That melts the lionhead's heel and horseshoe of the heart,
A brute land in the cool top of the country days
To trot with a loud mate the haybeds of a mile,
Love and labour and kill
In quick, sweet, cruel light till the locked ground sprout out,
The black, burst sea rejoice,
The bowels turn turtle,
Claw of the crabbed veins squeeze from each red particle
The parched and raging voice?

Fishermen of mermen
Creep and harp on the tide, sinking their charmed, bent pin
With bridebait of gold bread, I with a living skein,
Tongue and ear in the thread, angle the temple-bound
Curl-locked and animal cavepools of spells and bone,
Trace out a tentacle,
Nailed with an open eye, in the bowl of wounds and weed
To clasp my fury on ground
And clap its great blood down;
Never shall beast be born to atlas the few seas
Or poise the day on a horn.

Sigh long, clay cold, lie shorn,
Cast high, stunned on gilled stone; sly scissors ground in frost
Clack through the thicket of strength, love hewn in pillars
    drops
With carved bird, saint, and sun, the wrackspiked maiden
    mouth
Lops, as a bush plumed with flames, the rant of the fierce eye,
Clips short the gesture of breath.
Die in red feathers when the flying heaven's cut,
And roll with the knocked earth:
Lie dry, rest robbed, my beast.
You have kicked from a dark den, leaped up the whinnying
    light,
And dug your grave in my breast.

[101]

SONORA HIGH SCHOOL
LIBRARY

The tombstone told when she died.
Her two surnames stopped me still.
A virgin married at rest.
She married in this pouring place,
That I struck one day by luck,
Before I heard in my mother's side
Or saw in the looking-glass shell
The rain through her cold heart speak
And the sun killed in her face.
More the thick stone cannot tell.
Before she lay on a stranger's bed
With a hand plunged through her hair,
Or that rainy tongue beat back
Through the devilish years and innocent deaths
To the room of a secret child,
Among men later I heard it said
She cried her white-dressed limbs were bare
And her red lips were kissed black,
She wept in her pain and made mouths,
Talked and tore though her eyes smiled.

I who saw in a hurried film
Death and this mad heroine
Meet once on a mortal wall
Heard her speak through the chipped beak
Of the stone bird guarding her:
I died before bedtime came
But my womb was bellowing
And I felt with my bare fall
A blazing red harsh head tear up
And the dear floods of his hair.

On no work of words now for three lean months in the
    bloody
Belly of the rich year and the big purse of my body
I bitterly take to task my poverty and craft:

To take to give is all, return what is hungrily given
Puffing the pounds of manna up through the dew to heaven,
The lovely gift of the gab bangs back on a blind shaft.

To lift to leave from the treasures of man is pleasing death
That will rake at last all currencies of the marked breath
And count the taken, forsaken mysteries in a bad dark.

To surrender now is to pay the expensive ogre twice.
Ancient woods of my blood, dash down to the nut of the seas
If I take to burn or return this world which is each man's
    work.

A saint about to fall,
The stained flats of heaven hit and razed
To the kissed kite hems of his shawl,
On the last street wave praised
The unwinding, song by rock,
Of the woven wall
Of his father's house in the sands,
The vanishing of the musical ship-work and the chucked bells,
The wound-down cough of the blood-counting clock
Behind a face of hands,
On the angelic etna of the last whirring featherlands,
Wind-heeled foot in the hole of a fireball,
Hymned his shrivelling flock,
On the last rick's tip by spilled wine-wells
Sang heaven hungry and the quick
Cut Christbread spitting vinegar and all
The mazes of his praise and envious tongue were worked in
        flames and shells.

Glory cracked like a flea.
The sun-leaved holy candlewoods
Drivelled down to one singeing tree
With a stub of black buds,
The sweet, fish-gilled boats bringing blood
Lurched through a scuttled sea
With a hold of leeches and straws,
Heaven fell with his fall and one crocked bell beat the left air.

O wake in me in my house in the mud
Of the crotch of the squawking shores,
Flicked from the carbolic city puzzle in a bed of sores
The scudding base of the familiar sky,
The lofty roots of the clouds.
From an odd room in a split house stare,
Milk in your mouth, at the sour floods
That bury the sweet street slowly, see
The skull of the earth is barbed with a war of burning brains
    and hair.

Strike in the time-bomb town,
Raise the live rafters of the eardrum,
Throw your fear a parcel of stone
Through the dark asylum,
Lapped among herods wail
As their blade marches in
That the eyes are already murdered,
The stocked heart is forced, and agony has another mouth to
    feed.

O wake to see, after a noble fall,
The old mud hatch again, the horrid
Woe drip from the dishrag hands and the pressed sponge of
    the forehead,
The breath draw back like a bolt through white oil
And a stranger enter like iron.
Cry joy that this witchlike midwife second
Bullies into rough seas you so gentle
And makes with a flick of the thumb and sun
A thundering bullring of your silent and girl-circled island.

'If my head hurt a hair's foot
Pack back the downed bone. If the unpricked ball of my
       breath
Bump on a spout let the bubbles jump out.
Sooner drop with the worm of the ropes round my throat
Than bully ill love in the clouted scene.

'All game phrases fit your ring of a cockfight:
I'll comb the snared woods with a glove on a lamp,
Peck, sprint, dance on fountains and duck time
Before I rush in a crouch the ghost with a hammer, air,
Strike light, and bloody a loud room.

'If my bunched, monkey coming is cruel
Rage me back to the making house. My hand unravel
When you sew the deep door. The bed is a cross place.
Bend, if my journey ache, direction like an arc or make
A limp and riderless shape to leap nine thinning months.'

'No. Not for Christ's dazzling bed
Or a nacreous sleep among soft particles and charms
My dear would I change my tears or your iron head.
Thrust, my daughter or son, to escape, there is none, none,
       none,
Nor when all ponderous heaven's host of waters breaks.

'Now to awake husked of gestures and my joy like a cave
To the anguish and carrion, to the infant forever unfree,
O my lost love bounced from a good home;
The grain that hurries this way from the rim of the grave
Has a voice and a house, and there and here you must couch
    and cry.

'Rest beyond choice in the dust-appointed grain,
At the breast stored with seas. No return
Through the waves of the fat streets nor the skeleton's thin
    ways.
The grave and my calm body are shut to your coming as stone,
And the endless beginning of prodigies suffers open.'

Twenty-four years remind the tears of my eyes.
(Bury the dead for fear that they walk to the grave in labour.)
In the groin of the natural doorway I crouched like a tailor
Sewing a shroud for a journey
By the light of the meat-eating sun.
Dressed to die, the sensual strut begun,
With my red veins full of money,
In the final direction of the elementary town
I advance for as long as forever is.

The conversation of prayers about to be said
By the child going to bed and the man on the stairs
Who climbs to his dying love in her high room,
The one not caring to whom in his sleep he will move
And the other full of tears that she will be dead,

Turns in the dark on the sound they know will arise
Into the answering skies from the green ground,
From the man on the stairs and the child by his bed.
The sound about to be said in the two prayers
For the sleep in a safe land and the love who dies

Will be the same grief flying. Whom shall they calm?
Shall the child sleep unharmed or the man be crying?
The conversation of prayers about to be said
Turns on the quick and the dead, and the man on the stairs
To-night shall find no dying but alive and warm

In the fire of his care his love in the high room.
And the child not caring to whom he climbs his prayer
Shall drown in a grief as deep as his made grave,
And mark the dark eyed wave, through the eyes of sleep,
Dragging him up the stairs to one who lies dead.

Never until the mankind making
Bird beast and flower
Fathering and all humbling darkness
Tells with silence the last light breaking
And the still hour
Is come of the sea tumbling in harness

And I must enter again the round
Zion of the water bead
And the synagogue of the ear of corn
Shall I let pray the shadow of a sound
Or sow my salt seed
In the least valley of sackcloth to mourn

The majesty and burning of the child's death.
I shall not murder
The mankind of her going with a grave truth
Nor blaspheme down the stations of the breath
With any further
Elegy of innocence and youth.

Deep with the first dead lies London's daughter,
Robed in the long friends,
The grains beyond age, the dark veins of her mother,
Secret by the unmourning water
Of the riding Thames.
After the first death, there is no other.

It was my thirtieth year to heaven
Woke to my hearing from harbour and neighbour wood
  And the mussel pooled and the heron
        Priested shore
      The morning beckon
With water praying and call of seagull and rook
And the knock of sailing boats on the net webbed wall
      Myself to set foot
        That second
In the still sleeping town and set forth.

  My birthday began with the water-
Birds and the birds of the winged trees flying my name
  Above the farms and the white horses
        And I rose
      In rainy autumn
And walked abroad in a shower of all my days.
High tide and the heron dived when I took the road
      Over the border
        And the gates
Of the town closed as the town awoke.

  A springful of larks in a rolling
Cloud and the roadside bushes brimming with whistling
  Blackbirds and the sun of October
        Summery
      On the hill's shoulder,

Here were fond climates and sweet singers suddenly
Come in the morning where I wandered and listened
        To the rain wringing
           Wind blow cold
      In the wood faraway under me.

      Pale rain over the dwindling harbour
And over the sea wet church the size of a snail
        With its horns through mist and the castle
            Brown as owls
        But all the gardens
Of spring and summer were blooming in the tall tales
Beyond the border and under the lark full cloud.
        There could I marvel
          My birthday
Away but the weather turned around.

      It turned away from the blithe country
And down the other air and the blue altered sky
        Streamed again a wonder of summer
            With apples
        Pears and red currants
And I saw in the turning so clearly a child's
Forgotten mornings when he walked with his mother
        Through the parables
          Of sun light
And the legends of the green chapels

And the twice told fields of infancy
That his tears burned my cheeks and his heart moved in mine.
　　　These were the woods the river and sea
　　　　　　Where a boy
　　　　　　In the listening
Summertime of the dead whispered the truth of his joy
To the trees and the stones and the fish in the tide.
　　　　　　And the mystery
　　　　　　Sang alive
Still in the water and singingbirds.

And there could I marvel my birthday
Away but the weather turned around. And the true
　　　Joy of the long dead child sang burning
　　　　　　In the sun.
　　　　　　It was my thirtieth
Year to heaven stood there then in the summer noon
Though the town below lay leaved with October blood.
　　　　　　O may my heart's truth
　　　　　　Still be sung
On this high hill in a year's turning.

THIS SIDE OF THE TRUTH
(for Llewelyn)

This side of the truth,
You may not see, my son,
King of your blue eyes
In the blinding country of youth,
That all is undone,
Under the unminding skies,
Of innocence and guilt
Before you move to make
One gesture of the heart or head,
Is gathered and spilt
Into the winding dark
Like the dust of the dead.

Good and bad, two ways
Of moving about your death
By the grinding sea,
King of your heart in the blind days,
Blow away like breath,
Go crying through you and me
And the souls of all men
Into the innocent
Dark, and the guilty dark, and good
Death, and bad death, and then
In the last element
Fly like the stars' blood,

Like the sun's tears,
Like the moon's seed, rubbish
And fire, the flying rant
Of the sky, king of your six years.
And the wicked wish,
Down the beginning of plants
And animals and birds,
Water and light, the earth and sky,
Is cast before you move,
And all your deeds and words,
Each truth, each lie,
Die in unjudging love.

Friend by enemy I call you out.

You with a bad coin in your socket,
You my friend there with a winning air
Who palmed the lie on me when you looked
Brassily at my shyest secret,
Enticed with twinkling bits of the eye
Till the sweet tooth of my love bit dry,
Rasped at last, and I stumbled and sucked,
Whom now I conjure to stand as thief
In the memory worked by mirrors,
With unforgettably smiling act,
Quickness of hand in the velvet glove
And my whole heart under your hammer,
Were once such a creature, so gay and frank
A desireless familiar
I never thought to utter or think
While you displaced a truth in the air,

That though I loved them for their faults
As much as for their good,
My friends were enemies on stilts
With their heads in a cunning cloud.

A stranger has come
To share my room in the house not right in the head,
A girl mad as birds

Bolting the night of the door with her arm her plume.
Strait in the mazed bed
She deludes the heaven-proof house with entering clouds

Yet she deludes with walking the nightmarish room,
At large as the dead,
Or rides the imagined oceans of the male wards.

She has come possessed
Who admits the delusive light through the bouncing wall,
Possessed by the skies

She sleeps in the narrow trough yet she walks the dust
Yet raves at her will
On the madhouse boards worn thin by my walking tears.

And taken by light in her arms at long and dear last
I may without fail
Suffer the first vision that set fire to the stars.

Unluckily for a death
Waiting with phoenix under
The pyre yet to be lighted of my sins and days,
And for the woman in shades
Saint carved and sensual among the scudding
Dead and gone, dedicate forever to my self
Though the brawl of the kiss has not occurred
On the clay cold mouth, on the fire
Branded forehead, that could bind
Her constant, nor the winds of love broken wide
To the wind the choir and cloister
Of the wintry nunnery of the order of lust
Beneath my life, that sighs for the seducer's coming
In the sun strokes of summer,

Loving on this sea banged guilt
My holy lucky body
Under the cloud against love is caught and held and kissed
In the mill of the midst
Of the descending day, the dark our folly
Cut to the still star in the order of the quick
But blessed by such heroic hosts in your every
Inch and glance that the wound
Is certain god, and the ceremony of souls
Is celebrated there, and communion between suns.
Never shall my self chant
About the saint in shades while the endless breviary

Turns of your prayed flesh, nor shall I shoo the bird below
    me:
The death biding two lie lonely.

I see the tigron in tears
In the androgynous dark,
His striped and noon maned tribe striding to holocaust,
The she mules bear their minotaurs,
The duck-billed platypus broody in a milk of birds.
I see the wanting nun saint carved in a garb
Of shades, symbol of desire beyond my hours
And guilts, great crotch and giant
Continence. I see the unfired phoenix, herald
And heaven crier, arrow now of aspiring
And the renouncing of islands.
All love but for the full assemblage in flower
Of the living flesh is monstrous or immortal,
And the grave its daughters.

Love, my fate got luckily,
Teaches with no telling
That the phoenix' bid for heaven and the desire after
Death in the carved nunnery
Both shall fail if I bow not to your blessing
Nor walk in the cool of your mortal garden
With immortality at my side like Christ the sky.
This I know from the native

Tongue of your translating eyes. The young stars told me,
Hurling into beginning like Christ the child.
Lucklessly she must lie patient
And the vaulting bird be still. O my true love, hold me.
In your every inch and glance is the globe of genesis spun,
And the living earth your sons.

The hunchback in the park
A solitary mister
Propped between trees and water
From the opening of the garden lock
That lets the trees and water enter
Until the Sunday sombre bell at dark

Eating bread from a newspaper
Drinking water from the chained cup
That the children filled with gravel
In the fountain basin where I sailed my ship
Slept at night in a dog kennel
But nobody chained him up.

Like the park birds he came early
Like the water he sat down
And Mister they called Hey mister
The truant boys from the town
Running when he had heard them clearly
On out of sound

Past lake and rockery
Laughing when he shook his paper
Hunchbacked in mockery
Through the loud zoo of the willow groves
Dodging the park keeper
With his stick that picked up leaves.

And the old dog sleeper
Alone between nurses and swans
While the boys among willows
Made the tigers jump out of their eyes
To roar on the rockery stones
And the groves were blue with sailors

Made all day until bell time
A woman figure without fault
Straight as a young elm
Straight and tall from his crooked bones
That she might stand in the night
After the locks and chains

All night in the unmade park
After the railings and shrubberies
The birds the grass the trees the lake
And the wild boys innocent as strawberries
Had followed the hunchback
To his kennel in the dark.

I

Into her lying down head
His enemies entered bed,
Under the encumbered eyelid,
Through the rippled drum of the hair-buried ear;
And Noah's rekindled now unkind dove
Flew man-bearing there.
Last night in a raping wave
Whales unreined from the green grave
In fountains of origin gave up their love,
Along her innocence glided
Juan aflame and savagely young King Lear,
Queen Catherine howling bare
And Samson drowned in his hair,
The colossal intimacies of silent
Once seen strangers or shades on a stair;
There the dark blade and wanton sighing her down
To a haycock couch and the scythes of his arms
Rode and whistled a hundred times
Before the crowing morning climbed;
Man was the burning England she was sleep-walking, and the
enamouring island
Made her limbs blind by luminous charms,
Sleep to a newborn sleep in a swaddling loin-leaf stroked and
sang
And his runaway beloved childlike laid in the acorned
sand.

[125]

There where a numberless tongue
Wound their room with a male moan,
His faith around her flew undone
And darkness hung the walls with baskets of snakes,
A furnace-nostrilled column-membered
Super-or-near man
Resembling to her dulled sense
The thief of adolescence,
Early imaginary half remembered
Oceanic lover alone
Jealousy cannot forget for all her sakes,
Made his bad bed in her good
Night, and enjoyed as he would.
Crying, white gowned, from the middle moonlit stages
Out to the tiered and hearing tide,
Close and far she announced the theft of the heart
In the taken body at many ages,
Trespasser and broken bride
Celebrating at her side
All blood-signed assailings and vanished marriages in which
he had no lovely part
Nor could share, for his pride, to the least
Mutter and foul wingbeat of the solemnizing nightpriest
Her holy unholy hours with the always anonymous beast.

Two sand grains together in bed,
Head to heaven-circling head,
Singly lie with the whole wide shore,
The covering sea their nightfall with no names;
And out of every domed and soil-based shell
One voice in chains declaims
The female, deadly, and male
Libidinous betrayal,
Golden dissolving under the water veil.

A she bird sleeping brittle by
Her lover's wings that fold to-morrow's flight,
Within the nested treefork
Sings to the treading hawk
Carrion, paradise, chirrup my bright yolk.
A blade of grass longs with the meadow,
A stone lies lost and locked in the lark-high hill.
Open as to the air to the naked shadow
O she lies alone and still,
Innocent between two wars,
With the incestuous secret brother in the seconds to perpetuate the stars,
A man torn up mourns in the sole night.
And the second comers, the severers, the enemies from the deep
Forgotten dark, rest their pulse and bury their dead in her faithless sleep.

Do not go gentle into that good night,
Old age should burn and rave at close of day;
Rage, rage against the dying of the light.

Though wise men at their end know dark is right,
Because their words had forked no lightning they
Do not go gentle into that good night.

Good men, the last wave by, crying how bright
Their frail deeds might have danced in a green bay,
Rage, rage against the dying of the light.

Wild men who caught and sang the sun in flight,
And learn, too late, they grieved it on its way,
Do not go gentle into that good night.

Grave men, near death, who see with blinding sight
Blind eyes could blaze like meteors and be gay,
Rage, rage against the dying of the light.

And you, my father, there on the sad height,
Curse, bless, me now with your fierce tears, I pray.
Do not go gentle into that good night.
Rage, rage against the dying of the light.

On almost the incendiary eve
    Of several near deaths,
When one at the great least of your best loved
    And always known must leave
Lions and fires of his flying breath,
    Of your immortal friends
Who'd raise the organs of the counted dust
    To shoot and sing your praise,
One who called deepest down shall hold his peace
    That cannot sink or cease
    Endlessly to his wound
In many married London's estranging grief.

On almost the incendiary eve
    When at your lips and keys,
Locking, unlocking, the murdered strangers weave,
    One who is most unknown,
Your polestar neighbour, sun of another street,
    Will dive up to his tears.
He'll bathe his raining blood in the male sea
    Who strode for your own dead
And wind his globe out of your water thread
    And load the throats of shells
    With every cry since light
Flashed first across his thunderclapping eyes.

On almost the incendiary eve
   Of deaths and entrances,
When near and strange wounded on London's waves
   Have sought your single grave,
One enemy, of many, who knows well
   Your heart is luminous
In the watched dark, quivering through locks and caves,
   Will pull the thunderbolts
To shut the sun, plunge, mount your darkened keys
   And sear just riders back,
      Until that one loved least
Looms the last Samson of your zodiac.

It is a winter's tale
That the snow blind twilight ferries over the lakes
And floating fields from the farm in the cup of the vales,
Gliding windless through the hand folded flakes,
The pale breath of cattle at the stealthy sail,

And the stars falling cold,
And the smell of hay in the snow, and the far owl
Warning among the folds, and the frozen hold
Flocked with the sheep white smoke of the farm house cowl
In the river wended vales where the tale was told.

Once when the world turned old
On a star of faith pure as the drifting bread,
As the food and flames of the snow, a man unrolled
The scrolls of fire that burned in his heart and head,
Torn and alone in a farm house in a fold

Of fields. And burning then
In his firelit island ringed by the winged snow
And the dung hills white as wool and the hen
Roosts sleeping chill till the flame of the cock crow
Combs through the mantled yards and the morning men

Stumble out with their spades,
The cattle stirring, the mousing cat stepping shy,
The puffed birds hopping and hunting, the milkmaids
Gentle in their clogs over the fallen sky,
And all the woken farm at its white trades,

He knelt, he wept, he prayed,
By the spit and the black pot in the log bright light
And the cup and the cut bread in the dancing shade,
In the muffled house, in the quick of night,
At the point of love, forsaken and afraid.

He knelt on the cold stones,
He wept from the crest of grief, he prayed to the veiled sky
May his hunger go howling on bare white bones
Past the statues of the stables and the sky roofed sties
And the duck pond glass and the blinding byres alone

Into the home of prayers
And fires where he should prowl down the cloud
Of his snow blind love and rush in the white lairs.
His naked need struck him howling and bowed
Though no sound flowed down the hand folded air

But only the wind strung
Hunger of birds in the fields of the bread of water, tossed
In high corn and the harvest melting on their tongues.
And his nameless need bound him burning and lost
When cold as snow he should run the wended vales among

The rivers mouthed in night,
And drown in the drifts of his need, and lie curled caught
In the always desiring centre of the white
Inhuman cradle and the bride bed forever sought
By the believer lost and the hurled outcast of light.

Deliver him, he cried,
By losing him all in love, and cast his need
Alone and naked in the engulfing bride,
Never to flourish in the fields of the white seed
Or flower under the time dying flesh astride.

Listen. The minstrels sing
In the departed villages. The nightingale,
Dust in the buried wood, flies on the grains of her wings
And spells on the winds of the dead his winter's tale.
The voice of the dust of water from the withered spring

Is telling. The wizened
Stream with bells and baying water bounds. The dew rings
On the gristed leaves and the long gone glistening
Parish of snow. The carved mouths in the rock are wind
    swept strings.
Time sings through the intricately dead snow drop. Listen.

It was a hand or sound
In the long ago land that glided the dark door wide
And there outside on the bread of the ground
A she bird rose and rayed like a burning bride.
A she bird dawned, and her breast with snow and scarlet
    downed.

Look. And the dancers move
On the departed, snow bushed green, wanton in moon light
As a dust of pigeons. Exulting, the grave hooved
Horses, centaur dead, turn and tread the drenched white
Paddocks in the farms of birds. The dead oak walks for love.

The carved limbs in the rock
Leap, as to trumpets. Calligraphy of the old
Leaves is dancing. Lines of age on the stones weave in a flock.
And the harp shaped voice of the water's dust plucks in a fold
Of fields. For love, the long ago she bird rises. Look.

And the wild wings were raised
Above her folded head, and the soft feathered voice
Was flying through the house as though the she bird praised
And all the elements of the slow fall rejoiced
That a man knelt alone in the cup of the vales,

In the mantle and calm,
By the spit and the black pot in the log bright light.
And the sky of birds in the plumed voice charmed
Him up and he ran like a wind after the kindling flight
Past the blind barns and byres of the windless farm.

In the poles of the year
When black birds died like priests in the cloaked hedge row
And over the cloth of counties the far hills rode near,
Under the one leaved trees ran a scarecrow of snow
And fast through the drifts of the thickets antlered like deer,

Rags and prayers down the knee-
Deep hillocks and loud on the numbed lakes,
All night lost and long wading in the wake of the she-
Bird through the times and lands and tribes of the slow flakes.
Listen and look where she sails the goose plucked sea,

The sky, the bird, the bride,
The cloud, the need, the planted stars, the joy beyond
The fields of seed and the time dying flesh astride,
The heavens, the heaven, the grave, the burning font.
In the far ago land the door of his death glided wide,

And the bird descended.
On a bread white hill over the cupped farm
And the lakes and floating fields and the river wended
Vales where he prayed to come to the last harm
And the home of prayers and fires, the tale ended.

The dancing perishes
On the white, no longer growing green, and, minstrel dead,
The singing breaks in the snow shoed villages of wishes
That once cut the figures of birds on the deep bread
And over the glazed lakes skated the shapes of fishes

Flying. The rite is shorn
Of nightingale and centaur dead horse. The springs wither
Back. Lines of age sleep on the stones till trumpeting dawn.
Exultation lies down. Time buries the spring weather
That belled and bounded with the fossil and the dew reborn.

For the bird lay bedded
In a choir of wings, as though she slept or died,
And the wings glided wide and he was hymned and wedded,
And through the thighs of the engulfing bride,
The woman breasted and the heaven headed

       Bird, he was brought low,
Burning in the bride bed of love, in the whirl-
Pool at the wanting centre, in the folds
Of paradise, in the spun bud of the world.
And she rose with him flowering in her melting snow.

The sky is torn across
This ragged anniversary of two
Who moved for three years in tune
Down the long walks of their vows.

Now their love lies a loss
And Love and his patients roar on a chain;
From every true or crater
Carrying cloud, Death strikes their house.

Too late in the wrong rain
They come together whom their love parted:
The windows pour into their heart
And the doors burn in their brain.

There was a saviour
    Rarer than radium,
Commoner than water, crueller than truth;
    Children kept from the sun
    Assembled at his tongue
To hear the golden note turn in a groove,
Prisoners of wishes locked their eyes
In the jails and studies of his keyless smiles.

    The voice of children says
    From a lost wilderness
There was calm to be done in his safe unrest,
    When hindering man hurt
    Man, animal, or bird
We hid our fears in that murdering breath,
Silence, silence to do, when earth grew loud,
In lairs and asylums of the tremendous shout.

    There was glory to hear
    In the churches of his tears,
Under his downy arm you sighed as he struck,
    O you who could not cry
    On to the ground when a man died
Put a tear for joy in the unearthly flood
And laid your cheek against a cloud-formed shell:
Now in the dark there is only yourself and myself.

Two proud, blacked brothers cry,
　　Winter-locked side by side,
To this inhospitable hollow year,
　　O we who could not stir
　　One lean sigh when we heard
Greed on man beating near and fire neighbour
　But wailed and nested in the sky-blue wall
Now break a giant tear for the little known fall,

　　For the drooping of homes
　　That did not nurse our bones,
Brave deaths of only ones but never found,
　　Now see, alone in us,
　　Our own true strangers' dust
Ride through the doors of our unentered house.
Exiled in us we arouse the soft,
Unclenched, armless, silk and rough love that breaks all rocks.

Waking alone in a multitude of loves when morning's light
Surprised in the opening of her nightlong eyes
His golden yesterday asleep upon the iris
And this day's sun leapt up the sky out of her thighs
Was miraculous virginity old as loaves and fishes,
Though the moment of a miracle is unending lightning
And the shipyards of Galilee's footprints hide a navy of doves.

No longer will the vibrations of the sun desire on
Her deepsea pillow where once she married alone,
Her heart all ears and eyes, lips catching the avalanche
Of the golden ghost who ringed with his streams her mercury
    bone,
Who under the lids of her windows hoisted his golden lug-
    gage,
For a man sleeps where fire leapt down and she learns through
    his arm
That other sun, the jealous coursing of the unrivalled blood.

In my craft or sullen art
Exercised in the still night
When only the moon rages
And the lovers lie abed
With all their griefs in their arms,
I labour by singing light
Not for ambition or bread
Or the strut and trade of charms
On the ivory stages
But for the common wages
Of their most secret heart.

Not for the proud man apart
From the raging moon I write
On these spindrift pages
Nor for the towering dead
With their nightingales and psalms
But for the lovers, their arms
Round the griefs of the ages,
Who pay no praise or wages
Nor heed my craft or art.

I

Myselves
The grievers
Grieve
Among the street burned to tireless death
A child of a few hours
With its kneading mouth
Charred on the black breast of the grave
The mother dug, and its arms full of fires.

Begin
With singing
Sing
Darkness kindled back into beginning
When the caught tongue nodded blind,
A star was broken
Into the centuries of the child
Myselves grieve now, and miracles cannot atone.

Forgive
Us forgive
Us your death that myselves the believers
May hold it in a great flood
Till the blood shall spurt,
And the dust shall sing like a bird
As the grains blow, as your death grows, through our heart.

[143]

Crying
Your dying
Cry,
Child beyond cockcrow, by the fire-dwarfed
Street we chant the flying sea
In the body bereft.
Love is the last light spoken. Oh
Seed of sons in the loin of the black husk left.

II

I know not whether
Adam or Eve, the adorned holy bullock
Or the white ewe lamb
Or the chosen virgin
Laid in her snow
On the altar of London,
Was the first to die
In the cinder of the little skull,
O bride and bride groom
O Adam and Eve together
Lying in the lull
Under the sad breast of the head stone
White as the skeleton
Of the garden of Eden.

I know the legend
Of Adam and Eve is never for a second
Silent in my service
Over the dead infants
Over the one
Child who was priest and servants,
Word, singers, and tongue
In the cinder of the little skull,
Who was the serpent's
Night fall and the fruit like a sun,
Man and woman undone,
Beginning crumbled back to darkness
Bare as the nurseries
Of the garden of wilderness.

III

Into the organpipes and steeples
Of the luminous cathedrals,
Into the weathercocks' molten mouths
Rippling in twelve-winded circles,
Into the dead clock burning the hour
Over the urn of sabbaths
Over the whirling ditch of daybreak
Over the sun's hovel and the slum of fire
And the golden pavements laid in requiems,
Into the bread in a wheatfield of flames,

Into the wine burning like brandy,
The masses of the sea
The masses of the sea under
The masses of the infant-bearing sea
Erupt, fountain, and enter to utter for ever
Glory glory glory
The sundering ultimate kingdom of genesis' thunder.

Once below a time,
When my pinned-around-the-spirit
Cut-to-measure flesh bit,
Suit for a serial sum
On the first of each hardship,
My paid-for slaved-for own too late
In love torn breeches and blistered jacket
On the snapping rims of the ashpit,
In grottoes I worked with birds,
Spiked with a mastiff collar,
Tasselled in cellar and snipping shop
Or decked on a cloud swallower,

Then swift from a bursting sea with bottlecork boats
And out-of-perspective sailors,
In common clay clothes disguised as scales,
As a he-god's paddling water skirts,
I astounded the sitting tailors,
I set back the clock faced tailors,
Then, bushily swanked in bear wig and tails,
Hopping hot leaved and feathered
From the kangaroo foot of the earth,
From the chill, silent centre
Trailing the frost bitten cloth,
Up through the lubber crust of Wales
I rocketed to astonish

The flashing needle rock of squatters,
The criers of Shabby and Shorten,
The famous stitch droppers.

II

My silly suit, hardly yet suffered for,
Around some coffin carrying
Birdman or told ghost I hung.
And the owl hood, the heel hider,
Claw fold and hole for the rotten
Head, deceived, I believed, my maker,

The cloud perched tailors' master with nerves for cotton.
On the old seas from stories, thrashing my wings,
Combing with antlers, Columbus on fire,
I was pierced by the idol tailor's eyes,
Glared through shark mask and navigating head,
Cold Nansen's beak on a boat full of gongs,

To the boy of common thread,
The bright pretender, the ridiculous sea dandy
With dry flesh and earth for adorning and bed.
It was sweet to drown in the readymade handy water
With my cherry capped dangler green as seaweed

Summoning a child's voice from a webfoot stone,
Never never oh never to regret the bugle I wore
On my cleaving arm as I blasted in a wave.
Now shown and mostly bare I would lie down,
Lie down, lie down and live
As quiet as a bone.

When I woke, the town spoke.
Birds and clocks and cross bells
Dinned aside the coiling crowd,
The reptile profligates in a flame,
Spoilers and pokers of sleep,
The next-door sea dispelled
Frogs and satans and woman-luck,
While a man outside with a billhook,
Up to his head in his blood,
Cutting the morning off,
The warm-veined double of Time
And his scarving beard from a book,
Slashed down the last snake as though
It were a wand or subtle bough,
Its tongue peeled in the wrap of a leaf.

Every morning I make,
God in bed, good and bad,
After a water-face walk,
The death-stagged scatter-breath
Mammoth and sparrowfall
Everybody's earth.
Where birds ride like leaves and boats like ducks

I heard, this morning, waking,
Crossly out of the town noises
A voice in the erected air,
No prophet-progeny of mine,
Cry my sea town was breaking.
No Time, spoke the clocks, no God, rang the bells,
I drew the white sheet over the islands
And the coins on my eyelids sang like shells.

When the morning was waking over the war
He put on his clothes and stepped out and he died,
The locks yawned loose and a blast blew them wide,
He dropped where he loved on the burst pavement stone
And the funeral grains of the slaughtered floor.
Tell his street on its back he stopped a sun
And the craters of his eyes grew springshoots and fire
When all the keys shot from the locks, and rang.
Dig no more for the chains of his grey-haired heart.
The heavenly ambulance drawn by a wound
Assembling waits for the spade's ring on the cage.
O keep his bones away from that common cart,
The morning is flying on the wings of his age
And a hundred storks perch on the sun's right hand.

Lie still, sleep becalmed, sufferer with the wound
In the throat, burning and turning. All night afloat
On the silent sea we have heard the sound
That came from the wound wrapped in the salt sheet.

Under the mile off moon we trembled listening
To the sea sound flowing like blood from the loud wound
And when the salt sheet broke in a storm of singing
The voices of all the drowned swam on the wind.

Open a pathway through the slow sad sail,
Throw wide to the wind the gates of the wandering boat
For my voyage to begin to the end of my wound,
We heard the sea sound sing, we saw the salt sheet tell.
Lie still, sleep becalmed, hide the mouth in the throat,
Or we shall obey, and ride with you through the drowned.

I

Who
Are you
Who is born
In the next room
So loud to my own
That I can hear the womb
Opening and the dark run
Over the ghost and the dropped son
Behind the wall thin as a wren's bone?
In the birth bloody room unknown
To the burn and turn of time
And the heart print of man
Bows no baptism
But dark alone
Blessing on
The wild
Child.

I
Must lie
Still as stone
By the wren bone
Wall hearing the moan
Of the mother hidden
And the shadowed head of pain
Casting to-morrow like a thorn
And the midwives of miracle sing
Until the turbulent new born
Burns me his name and his flame
And the winged wall is torn
By his torrid crown
And the dark thrown
From his loin
To bright
Light.

When
The wren
Bone writhes down
And the first dawn
Furied by his stream
Swarms on the kingdom come
Of the dazzler of heaven
And the splashed mothering maiden
Who bore him with a bonfire in
His mouth and rocked him like a storm
I shall run lost in sudden
Terror and shining from
The once hooded room
Crying in vain
In the caldron
Of his
Kiss

In
The spin
Of the sun
In the spuming
Cyclone of his wing
For I was lost who am
Crying at the man drenched throne
In the first fury of his stream
And the lightnings of adoration
Back to black silence melt and mourn
For I was lost who have come
To dumbfounding haven
And the finding one
And the high noon
Of his wound
Blinds my
Cry.

There
Crouched bare
In the shrine
Of his blazing
Breast I shall waken
To the judge blown bedlam
Of the uncaged sea bottom
The cloud climb of the exhaling tomb
And the bidden dust upsailing
With his flame in every grain.
O spiral of ascension
From the vultured urn
Of the morning
Of man when
The land
And

                    The
                  Born   sea
                Praised the sun
               The finding one
              And upright Adam
             Sang   upon   origin!
            O the wings of the children!
          The woundward flight of the ancient
        Young from the canyons of oblivion!
          The sky stride of the always slain
            In battle! the happening
              Of saints to their vision!
                The world winding home!
                And the whole pain
                  Flows open
                    And I
                    D i e .

II

In the name of the lost who glory in
The swinish plains of carrion
Under the burial song
Of the birds of burden
Heavy with the drowned
And the green dust
And bearing
The ghost
From
The ground
Like pollen
On the black plume
And the beak of slime
I pray though I belong
Not wholly to that lamenting
Brethren for joy has moved within
The inmost marrow of my heart bone

That he who learns now the sun and moon
Of his mother's milk may return
Before the lips blaze and bloom
To the birth bloody room
Behind the wall's wren
Bone and be dumb
And the womb
That bore
For
All men
The adored
Infant light or
The dazzling prison
Yawn to his upcoming.
In the name of the wanton
Lost on the unchristened mountain
In the centre of dark I pray him

That he let the dead lie though they moan
For his briared hands to hoist them
To the shrine of his world's wound
And the blood drop's garden
Endure the stone
Blind host to sleep
In the dark
And deep
Rock
Awake
No heart bone
But let it break
On the mountain crown
Unbidden by the sun
And the beating dust be blown
Down to the river rooting plain
Under the night forever falling.

Forever falling night is a known
Star and country to the legion
Of sleepers whose tongue I toll
To mourn his deluging
Light through sea and soil
And we have come
To know all
P l a c e s
Ways
M a z e s
P a s s a g e s
Quarters and graves
Of the endless fall.
Now common lazarus
Of the charting sleepers prays
Never to awake and arise
For the country of death is the heart's size

And the star of the lost the shape of the eyes.
In the name of the fatherless
In the name of the unborn
And the undesirers
Of midwiving morning's
Hands or instruments
O in the name
Of no one
Now or
No
One to
Be I pray
May the crimson
Sun spin a grave grey
And the colour of clay
Stream upon his martyrdom
In the interpreted evening
And the known dark of the earth amen.

I turn the corner of prayer and burn
In a blessing of the sudden
Sun. In the name of the damned
I would turn back and run
To the hidden land
But the loud sun
Christens down
The sky.
I
Am found.
O let him
Scald me and drown
Me in his world's wound.
His lightning answers my
Cry. My voice burns in his hand.
Now I am lost in the blinding
One. The sun roars at the prayer's end.

The bows glided down, and the coast
Blackened with birds took a last look
At his thrashing hair and whale-blue eye;
The trodden town rang its cobbles for luck.

Then good-bye to the fishermanned
Boat with its anchor free and fast
As a bird hooking over the sea,
High and dry by the top of the mast,

Whispered the affectionate sand
And the bulwarks of the dazzled quay.
For my sake sail, and never look back,
Said the looking land.

Sails drank the wind, and white as milk
He sped into the drinking dark;
The sun shipwrecked west on a pearl
And the moon swam out of its hulk.

Funnels and masts went by in a whirl.
Good-bye to the man on the sea-legged deck
To the gold gut that sings on his reel
To the bait that stalked out of the sack,

For we saw him throw to the swift flood
A girl alive with his hooks through her lips;
All the fishes were rayed in blood,
Said the dwindling ships.

Good-bye to chimneys and funnels,
Old wives that spin in the smoke,
He was blind to the eyes of candles
In the praying windows of waves

But heard his bait buck in the wake
And tussle in a shoal of loves.
Now cast down your rod, for the whole
Of the sea is hilly with whales,

She longs among horses and angels,
The rainbow-fish bend in her joys,
Floated the lost cathedral
Chimes of the rocked buoys.

Where the anchor rode like a gull
Miles over the moonstruck boat
A squall of birds bellowed and fell,
A cloud blew the rain from its throat;

He saw the storm smoke out to kill
With fuming bows and ram of ice,
Fire on starlight, rake Jesu's stream;
And nothing shone on the water's face

But the oil and bubble of the moon,
Plunging and piercing in his course
The lured fish under the foam
Witnessed with a kiss.

Whales in the wake like capes and Alps
Quaked the sick sea and snouted deep,
Deep the great bushed bait with raining lips
Slipped the fins of those humpbacked tons

And fled their love in a weaving dip.
Oh, Jericho was falling in their lungs!
She nipped and dived in the nick of love,
Spun on a spout like a long-legged ball

Till every beast blared down in a swerve
Till every turtle crushed from his shell
Till every bone in the rushing grave
Rose and crowed and fell!

Good luck to the hand on the rod,
There is thunder under its thumbs;
Gold gut is a lightning thread,
His fiery reel sings off its flames,

The whirled boat in the burn of his blood
Is crying from nets to knives,
Oh the shearwater birds and their boatsized brood
Oh the bulls of Biscay and their calves

Are making under the green, laid veil
The long-legged beautiful bait their wives.
Break the black news and paint on a sail
Huge weddings in the waves,

Over the wakeward-flashing spray
Over the gardens of the floor
Clash out the mounting dolphin's day,
My mast is a bell-spire,

Strike and smoothe, for my decks are drums,
Sing through the water-spoken prow
The octopus walking into her limbs
The polar eagle with his tread of snow.

From salt-lipped beak to the kick of the stern
Sing how the seal has kissed her dead!
The long, laid minute's bride drifts on
Old in her cruel bed.

Over the graveyard in the water
Mountains and galleries beneath
Nightingale and hyena
Rejoicing for that drifting death

Sing and howl through sand and anemone
Valley and sahara in a shell,
Oh all the wanting flesh his enemy
Thrown to the sea in the shell of a girl

Is old as water and plain as an eel;
Always good-bye to the long-legged bread
Scattered in the paths of his heels
For the salty birds fluttered and fed

And the tall grains foamed in their bills;
Always good-bye to the fires of the face,
For the crab-backed dead on the sea-bed rose
And scuttled over her eyes,

The blind, clawed stare is cold as sleet.
The tempter under the eyelid
Who shows to the selves asleep
Mast-high moon-white women naked

Walking in wishes and lovely for shame
Is dumb and gone with his flame of brides.
Sussanah's drowned in the bearded stream
And no-one stirs at Sheba's side

But the hungry kings of the tides;
Sin who had a woman's shape
Sleeps till Silence blows on a cloud
And all the lifted waters walk and leap.

Lucifer that bird's dropping
Out of the sides of the north
Has melted away and is lost
Is always lost in her vaulted breath,

Venus lies star-struck in her wound
And the sensual ruins make
Seasons over the liquid world,
White springs in the dark.

Always good-bye, cried the voices through the shell,
Good-bye always for the flesh is cast
And the fisherman winds his reel
With no more desire than a ghost.

Always good luck, praised the finned in the feather
Bird after dark and the laughing fish
As the sails drank up the hail of thunder
And the long-tailed lightning lit his catch.

The boat swims into the six-year weather,
A wind throws a shadow and it freezes fast.
See what the gold gut drags from under
Mountains and galleries to the crest!

See what clings to hair and skull
As the boat skims on with drinking wings!
The statues of great rain stand still,
And the flakes fall like hills.

Sing and strike his heavy haul
Toppling up the boatside in a snow of light!
His decks are drenched with miracles.
Oh miracle of fishes! The long dead bite!

Out of the urn the size of a man
Out of the room the weight of his trouble
Out of the house that holds a town
In the continent of a fossil

One by one in dust and shawl,
Dry as echoes and insect-faced,
His fathers cling to the hand of the girl
And the dead hand leads the past,

Leads them as children and as air
On to the blindly tossing tops;
The centuries throw back their hair
And the old men sing from newborn lips:

Time is bearing another son.
Kill Time! She turns in her pain!
The oak is felled in the acorn
And the hawk in the egg kills the wren.

He who blew the great fire in
And died on a hiss of flames
Or walked on the earth in the evening
Counting the denials of the grains

Clings to her drifting hair, and climbs;
And he who taught their lips to sing
Weeps like the risen sun among
The liquid choirs of his tribes.

The rod bends low, divining land,
And through the sundered water crawls
A garden holding to her hand
With birds and animals

With men and women and waterfalls
Trees cool and dry in the whirlpool of ships
And stunned and still on the green, laid veil
Sand with legends in its virgin laps

And prophets loud on the burned dunes;
Insects and valleys hold her thighs hard,
Time and places grip her breast bone,
She is breaking with seasons and clouds;

Round her trailed wrist fresh water weaves,
With moving fish and rounded stones
Up and down the greater waves
A separate river breathes and runs;

Strike and sing his catch of fields
For the surge is sown with barley,
The cattle graze on the covered foam,
The hills have footed the waves away,

With wild sea fillies and soaking bridles
With salty colts and gales in their limbs
All the horses of his haul of miracles
Gallop through the arched, green farms,

Trot and gallop with gulls upon them
And thunderbolts in their manes.
O Rome and Sodom To-morrow and London
The country tide is cobbled with towns,

And steeples pierce the cloud on her shoulder
And the streets that the fisherman combed
When his long-legged flesh was a wind on fire
And his loin was a hunting flame

Coil from the thoroughfares of her hair
And terribly lead him home alive
Lead her prodigal home to his terror,
The furious ox-killing house of love.

Down, down, down, under the ground,
Under the floating villages,
Turns the moon-chained and water-wound
Metropolis of fishes,

There is nothing left of the sea but its sound,
Under the earth the loud sea walks,
In deathbeds of orchards the boat dies down
And the bait is drowned among hayricks,

Land, land, land, nothing remains
Of the pacing, famous sea but its speech,
And into its talkative seven tombs
The anchor dives through the floors of a church.

Good-bye, good luck, struck the sun and the moon,
To the fisherman lost on the land.
He stands alone at the door of his home,
With his long-legged heart in his hand.

O
Out of a bed of love
When that immortal hospital made one more move to soothe
The cureless counted body,
And ruin and his causes
Over the barbed and shooting sea assumed an army
And swept into our wounds and houses,
I climb to greet the war in which I have no heart but only
That one dark I owe my light,
Call for confessor and wiser mirror but there is none
To glow after the god stoning night
And I am struck as lonely as a holy maker by the sun.

No
Praise that the spring time is all
Gabriel and radiant shrubbery as the morning grows joyful
Out of the woebegone pyre
And the multitude's sultry tear turns cool on the weeping
wall,
My arising prodigal
Sun the father his quiver full of the infants of pure fire,
But blessed be hail and upheaval
That uncalm still it is sure alone to stand and sing
Alone in the husk of man's home
And the mother and toppling house of the holy spring,
If only for a last time.

Now as I was young and easy under the apple boughs
About the lilting house and happy as the grass was green,
    The night above the dingle starry,
      Time let me hail and climb
    Golden in the heydays of his eyes,
And honoured among wagons I was prince of the apple towns
And once below a time I lordly had the trees and leaves
      Trail with daisies and barley
    Down the rivers of the windfall light.

And as I was green and carefree, famous among the barns
About the happy yard and singing as the farm was home,
    In the sun that is young once only,
      Time let me play and be
    Golden in the mercy of his means,
And green and golden I was huntsman and herdsman, the
          calves
Sang to my horn, the foxes on the hills barked clear and cold,
      And the sabbath rang slowly
    In the pebbles of the holy streams.

All the sun long it was running, it was lovely, the hay
Fields high as the house, the tunes from the chimneys, it
        was air
    And playing, lovely and watery
      And fire green as grass.

And nightly under the simple stars
As I rode to sleep the owls were bearing the farm away,
All the moon long I heard, blessed among stables, the night-
jars
Flying with the ricks, and the horses
Flashing into the dark.

And then to awake, and the farm, like a wanderer white
With the dew, come back, the cock on his shoulder: it was all
Shining, it was Adam and maiden,
The sky gathered again
And the sun grew round that very day.
So it must have been after the birth of the simple light
In the first, spinning place, the spellbound horses walking
warm
Out of the whinnying green stable
On to the fields of praise.

And honoured among foxes and pheasants by the gay house
Under the new made clouds and happy as the heart was long,
In the sun born over and over,
I ran my heedless ways,
My wishes raced through the house high hay
And nothing I cared, at my sky blue trades, that time allows
In all his tuneful turning so few and such morning songs
Before the children green and golden
Follow him out of grace,

Nothing I cared, in the lamb white days, that time would
                    take me
Up to the swallow thronged loft by the shadow of my hand,
          In the moon that is always rising,
                    Nor that riding to sleep
          I should hear him fly with the high fields
And wake to the farm forever fled from the childless land.
Oh as I was young and easy in the mercy of his means,
                    Time held me green and dying
          Though I sang in my chains like the sea.

I

Never and never, my girl riding far and near
In the land of the hearthstone tales, and spelled asleep,
Fear or believe that the wolf in a sheepwhite hood
Loping and bleating roughly and blithely shall leap,

My dear, my dear,

Out of a lair in the flocked leaves in the dew dipped year
To eat your heart in the house in the rosy wood.

Sleep, good, for ever, slow and deep, spelled rare and wise,
My girl ranging the night in the rose and shire
Of the hobnail tales: no gooseherd or swine will turn
Into a homestall king or hamlet of fire

And prince of ice

To court the honeyed heart from your side before sunrise
In a spinney of ringed boys and ganders, spike and burn,

Nor the innocent lie in the rooting dingle wooed
And staved, and riven among plumes my rider weep.
From the broomed witch's spume you are shielded by fern
And flower of country sleep and the greenwood keep.

Lie fast and soothed,

Safe be and smooth from the bellows of the rushy brood.
Never, my girl, until tolled to sleep by the stern

Bell believe or fear that the rustic shade or spell
Shall harrow and snow the blood while you ride wide and
near,

[181]

For who unmanningly haunts the mountain ravened eaves
Or skulks in the dell moon but moonshine echoing clear
                                        From the starred well?
A hill touches an angel! Out of a saint's cell
The nightbird lauds through nunneries and domes of leaves

Her robin breasted tree, three Marys in the rays.
Sanctum sanctorum the animal eye of the wood
In the rain telling its beads, and the gravest ghost
The owl at its knelling. Fox and holt kneel before blood.
                                        Now the tales praise
The star rise at pasture and nightlong the fables graze
On the lord's-table of the bowing grass. Fear most

For ever of all not the wolf in his baaing hood
Nor the tusked prince, in the ruttish farm, at the rind
And mire of love, but the Thief as meek as the dew.
The country is holy: O bide in that country kind,
                                        Know the green good,
Under the prayer wheeling moon in the rosy wood
Be shielded by chant and flower and gay may you

Lie in grace. Sleep spelled at rest in the lowly house
In the squirrel nimble grove, under linen and thatch
And star: held and blessed, though you scour the high four
Winds, from the dousing shade and the roarer at the latch,
                                        Cool in your vows.
Yet out of the beaked, web dark and the pouncing boughs
Be you sure the Thief will seek a way sly and sure

And sly as snow and meek as dew blown to the thorn,
This night and each vast night until the stern bell talks
In the tower and tolls to sleep over the stalls
Of the hearthstone tales my own, lost love; and the soul
    walks
                                    The waters shorn.
This night and each night since the falling star you were born,
Ever and ever he finds a way, as the snow falls,

As the rain falls, hail on the fleece, as the vale mist rides
Through the haygold stalls, as the dew falls on the wind-
Milled dust of the apple tree and the pounded islands
Of the morning leaves, as the star falls, as the winged
                                    Apple seed glides,
And falls, and flowers in the yawning wound at our sides,
As the world falls, silent as the cyclone of silence.

Night and the reindeer on the clouds above the haycocks
And the wings of the great roc ribboned for the fair!
The leaping saga of prayer! And high, there, on the hare-
                                                Heeled winds the rooks
Cawing from their black bethels soaring, the holy books
Of birds! Among the cocks like fire the red fox

Burning! Night and the vein of birds in the winged, sloe
        wrist
Of the wood! Pastoral beat of blood through the laced
        leaves!
The stream from the priest black wristed spinney and sleeves
                                        Of thistling frost
Of the nightingale's din and tale! The upgiven ghost
Of the dingle torn to singing and the surpliced

Hill of cypresses! The din and tale in the skimmed
Yard of the buttermilk rain on the pail! The sermon
Of blood! The bird loud vein! The saga from mermen
                                        To seraphim
Leaping! The gospel rooks! All tell, this night, of him
Who comes as red as the fox and sly as the heeled wind.

Illumination of music! the lulled black-backed
Gull, on the wave with sand in its eyes! And the foal moves
Through the shaken greensward lake, silent, on moonshod
    hooves,
                                    In the winds' wakes.
Music of elements, that a miracle makes!
Earth, air, water, fire, singing into the white act,

The haygold haired, my love asleep, and the rift blue
Eyed, in the haloed house, in her rareness and hilly
High riding, held and blessed and true, and so stilly
                                    Lying the sky
Might cross its planets, the bell weep, night gather her eyes,
The Thief fall on the dead like the willy nilly dew,

Only for the turning of the earth in her holy
Heart! Slyly, slowly, hearing the wound in her side go
Round the sun, he comes to my love like the designed snow,
                                    And truly he
Flows to the strand of flowers like the dew's ruly sea,
And surely he sails like the ship shape clouds. Oh he

Comes designed to my love to steal not her tide raking
Wound, nor her riding high, nor her eyes, nor kindled hair,
But her faith that each vast night and the saga of prayer
                                        He comes to take
Her faith that this last night for his unsacred sake
He comes to leave her in the lawless sun awaking

Naked and forsaken to grieve he will not come.
Ever and ever by all your vows believe and fear
My dear this night he comes and night without end my dear
                                        Since you were born:
And you shall wake, from country sleep, this dawn and each
    first dawn,
Your faith as deathless as the outcry of the ruled sun.

Over Sir John's hill,
The hawk on fire hangs still;
In a hoisted cloud, at drop of dusk, he pulls to his claws
And gallows, up the rays of his eyes the small birds of
     the bay
And the shrill child's play
Wars
Of the sparrows and such who swansing, dusk, in wrangling
     hedges.
And blithely they squawk
To fiery tyburn over the wrestle of elms until
The flash the noosed hawk
Crashes, and slowly the fishing holy stalking heron
In the river Towy below bows his tilted headstone.

Flash, and the plumes crack,
And a black cap of jack-
Daws Sir John's just hill dons, and again the gulled birds
     hare
To the hawk on fire, the halter height, over Towy's fins,
In a whack of wind.
There
Where the elegiac fisherbird stabs and paddles

In the pebbly dab-filled
Shallow and sedge, and 'dilly dilly,' calls the loft hawk,
'Come and be killed,'
I open the leaves of the water at a passage
Of psalms and shadows among the pincered sandcrabs
    prancing

And read, in a shell,
Death clear as a buoy's bell:
All praise of the hawk on fire in hawk-eyed dusk be sung,
When his viperish fuse hangs looped with flames under the
    brand
Wing, and blest shall
Young
Green chickens of the bay and bushes cluck, 'dilly dilly,
Come let us die.'
We grieve as the blithe birds, never again, leave shingle
    and elm,
The heron and I,
I young Aesop fabling to the near night by the dingle
Of eels, saint heron hymning in the shell-hung distant

Crystal harbour vale
Where the sea cobbles sail,
And wharves of water where the walls dance and the white
    cranes stilt.

It is the heron and I, under judging Sir John's elmed
Hill, tell-tale the knelled
Guilt
Of the led-astray birds whom God, for their breast of
    whistles,
Have mercy on,
God in his whirlwind silence save, who marks the sparrows
    hail,
For their souls' song.
Now the heron grieves in the weeded verge. Through
    windows
Of dusk and water I see the tilting whispering

Heron, mirrored, go,
As the snapt feathers snow,
Fishing in the tear of the Towy. Only a hoot owl
Hollows, a grassblade blown in cupped hands, in the looted
    elms
And no green cocks or hens
Shout
Now on Sir John's hill. The heron, ankling the scaly
Lowlands of the waves,
Makes all the music; and I who hear the tune of the slow,
Wear-willow river, grave,
Before the lunge of the night, the notes on this time-shaken
Stone for the sake of the souls of the slain birds sailing.

In the mustardseed sun,
By full tilt river and switchback sea
    Where the cormorants scud,
In his house on stilts high among beaks
    And palavers of birds
This sandgrain day in the bent bay's grave
    He celebrates and spurns
His driftwood thirty-fifth wind turned age;
    Herons spire and spear.

Under and round him go
Flounders, gulls, on their cold, dying trails,
    Doing what they are told,
Curlews aloud in the congered waves
    Work at their ways to death,
And the rhymer in the long tongued room,
    Who tolls his birthday bell,
Toils towards the ambush of his wounds;
    Herons, steeple stemmed, bless.

In the thistledown fall,
He sings towards anguish; finches fly
    In the claw tracks of hawks
On a seizing sky; small fishes glide
    Through wynds and shells of drowned
Ship towns to pastures of otters. He
    In his slant, racking house
And the hewn coils of his trade perceives
    Herons walk in their shroud,

[190]

The livelong river's robe
Of minnows wreathing around their prayer;
    And far at sea he knows,
Who slaves to his crouched, eternal end
    Under a serpent cloud,
Dolphins dive in their turnturtle dust,
    The rippled seals streak down
To kill and their own tide daubing blood
    Slides good in the sleek mouth.

    In a cavernous, swung
Wave's silence, wept white angelus knells.
    Thirty-five bells sing struck
On skull and scar where his loves lie wrecked,
    Steered by the falling stars.
And to-morrow weeps in a blind cage
    Terror will rage apart
Before chains break to a hammer flame
    And love unbolts the dark

    And freely he goes lost
In the unknown, famous light of great
    And fabulous, dear God.
Dark is a way and light is a place,
    Heaven that never was
Nor will be ever is always true,
    And, in that brambled void,
Plenty as blackberries in the woods
    The dead grow for His joy.

There he might wander bare
With the spirits of the horseshoe bay
    Or the stars' seashore dead,
Marrow of eagles, the roots of whales
    And wishbones of wild geese,
With blessed, unborn God and His Ghost,
    And every soul His priest,
Gulled and chanter in young Heaven's fold
    Be at cloud quaking peace,

    But dark is a long way.
He, on the earth of the night, alone
    With all the living, prays,
Who knows the rocketing wind will blow
    The bones out of the hills,
And the scythed boulders bleed, and the last
    Rage shattered waters kick
Masts and fishes to the still quick stars,
    Faithlessly unto Him

    Who is the light of old
And air shaped Heaven where souls grow wild
    As horses in the foam:
Oh, let me midlife mourn by the shrined
    And druid herons' vows
The voyage to ruin I must run,
    Dawn ships clouted aground,
Yet, though I cry with tumbledown tongue,
    Count my blessings aloud:

Four elements and five
Senses, and man a spirit in love
    Tangling through this spun slime
To his nimbus bell cool kingdom come
    And the lost, moonshine domes,
And the sea that hides his secret selves
    Deep in its black, base bones,
Lulling of spheres in the seashell flesh,
    And this last blessing most,

    That the closer I move
To death, one man through his sundered hulks,
    The louder the sun blooms
And the tusked, ramshackling sea exults;
    And every wave of the way
And gale I tackle, the whole world then,
    With more triumphant faith
Than ever was since the world was said,
    Spins its morning of praise,

    I hear the bouncing hills
Grow larked and greener at berry brown
    Fall and the dew larks sing
Taller this thunderclap spring, and how
    More spanned with angels ride
The mansouled fiery islands! Oh,
    Holier then their eyes,
And my shining men no more alone
    As I sail out to die.

When I was a windy boy and a bit
And the black spit of the chapel fold,
(Sighed the old ram rod, dying of women),
I tiptoed shy in the gooseberry wood,
The rude owl cried like a telltale tit,
I skipped in a blush as the big girls rolled
Ninepin down on the donkeys' common,
And on seesaw sunday nights I wooed
Whoever I would with my wicked eyes,
The whole of the moon I could love and leave
All the green leaved little weddings' wives
In the coal black bush and let them grieve.

When I was a gusty man and a half
And the black beast of the beetles' pews,
(Sighed the old ram rod, dying of bitches),
Not a boy and a bit in the wick-
Dipping moon and drunk as a new dropped calf,
I whistled all night in the twisted flues,
Midwives grew in the midnight ditches,
And the sizzling beds of the town cried, Quick!—
Whenever I dove in a breast high shoal,
Wherever I ramped in the clover quilts,
Whatsoever I did in the coal-
Black night, I left my quivering prints.

When I was a man you could call a man
And the black cross of the holy house,
(Sighed the old ram rod, dying of welcome),
Brandy and ripe in my bright, bass prime,
No springtailed tom in the red hot town
With every simmering woman his mouse
But a hillocky bull in the swelter
Of summer come in his great good time
To the sultry, biding herds, I said,
Oh, time enough when the blood creeps cold,
And I lie down but to sleep in bed,
For my sulking, skulking, coal black soul!

When I was a half of the man I was
And serve me right as the preachers warn,
(Sighed the old ram rod, dying of downfall),
No flailing calf or cat in a flame
Or hickory bull in milky grass
But a black sheep with a crumpled horn,
At last the soul from its foul mousehole
Slung pouting out when the limp time came;
And I gave my soul a blind, slashed eye,
Gristle and rind, and a roarers' life,
And I shoved it into the coal black sky
To find a woman's soul for a wife.

Now I am a man no more no more
And a black reward for a roaring life,
(Sighed the old ram rod, dying of strangers),
Tidy and cursed in my dove cooed room
I lie down thin and hear the good bells jaw—
For, oh, my soul found a sunday wife
In the coal black sky and she bore angels!
Harpies around me out of her womb!
Chastity prays for me, piety sings,
Innocence sweetens my last black breath,
Modesty hides my thighs in her wings,
And all the deadly virtues plague my death!

Through throats where many rivers meet, the curlews cry,
Under the conceiving moon, on the high chalk hill,
And there this night I walk in the white giant's thigh
Where barren as boulders women lie longing still

To labour and love though they lay down long ago.

Through throats where many rivers meet, the women pray,
Pleading in the waded bay for the seed to flow
Though the names on their weed grown stones are rained
    away,

And alone in the night's eternal, curving act
They yearn with tongues of curlews for the unconceived
And immemorial sons of the cudgelling, hacked

Hill. Who once in gooseskin winter loved all ice leaved
In the courters' lanes, or twined in the ox roasting sun
In the wains tonned so high that the wisps of the hay
Clung to the pitching clouds, or gay with any one
Young as they in the after milking moonlight lay

Under the lighted shapes of faith and their moonshade
Petticoats galed high, or shy with the rough riding boys,
Now clasp me to their grains in the gigantic glade,

Who once, green countries since, were a hedgerow of joys.
Time by, their dust was flesh the swineherd rooted sly,

Flared in the reek of the wiving sty with the rush
Light of his thighs, spreadeagle to the dunghill sky,
Or with their orchard man in the core of the sun's bush
Rough as cows' tongues and thrashed with brambles their
    buttermilk
Manes, under his quenchless summer barbed gold to the
    bone,

Or rippling soft in the spinney moon as the silk
And ducked and draked white lake that harps to a hail stone.

Who once were a bloom of wayside brides in the hawed
    house
And heard the lewd, wooed field flow to the coming frost,
The scurrying, furred small friars squeal, in the dowse
Of day, in the thistle aisles, till the white owl crossed

Their breast, the vaulting does roister, the horned bucks
    climb
Quick in the wood at love, where a torch of foxes foams,
All birds and beasts of the linked night uproar and chime

And the mole snout blunt under his pilgrimage of domes,
Or, butter fat goosegirls, bounced in a gambo bed,
Their breasts full of honey, under their gander king
Trounced by his wings in the hissing shippen, long dead
And gone that barley dark where their clogs danced in the
    spring,

And their firefly hairpins flew, and the ricks ran round—

(But nothing bore, no mouthing babe to the veined hives
Hugged, and barren and bare on Mother Goose's ground
They with the simple Jacks were a boulder of wives)—

Now curlew cry me down to kiss the mouths of their dust.

The dust of their kettles and clocks swings to and fro
Where the hay rides now or the bracken kitchens rust
As the arc of the billhooks that flashed the hedges low
And cut the birds' boughs that the minstrel sap ran red.
They from houses where the harvest kneels, hold me hard,
Who heard the tall bell sail down the Sundays of the dead
And the rain wring out its tongues on the faded yard,
Teach me the love that is evergreen after the fall leaved
Grave, after Belovéd on the grass gulfed cross is scrubbed
Off by the sun and Daughters no longer grieved
Save by their long desirers in the fox cubbed
Streets or hungering in the crumbled wood: to these
Hale dead and deathless do the women of the hill
Love for ever meridian through the courters' trees

And the daughters of darkness flame like Fawkes fires still.

Too proud to die; broken and blind he died
The darkest way, and did not turn away,
A cold kind man brave in his narrow pride

On that darkest day. Oh, forever may
He lie lightly, at last, on the last, crossed
Hill, under the grass, in love, and there grow

Young among the long flocks, and never lie lost
Or still all the numberless days of his death, though
Above all he longed for his mother's breast

Which was rest and dust, and in the kind ground
The darkest justice of death, blind and unblessed.
Let him find no rest but be fathered and found,

I prayed in the crouching room, by his blind bed,
In the muted house, one minute before
Noon, and night, and light. The rivers of the dead

Veined his poor hand I held, and I saw
Through his unseeing eyes to the roots of the sea.
(An old tormented man three-quarters blind,

I am not too proud to cry that He and he
Will never never go out of my mind.
All his bones crying, and poor in all but pain,

Being innocent, he dreaded that he died
Hating his God, but what he was was plain:
An old kind man brave in his burning pride.

The sticks of the house were his; his books he owned.
Even as a baby he had never cried;
Nor did he now, save to his secret wound.

Out of his eyes I saw the last light glide.
Here among the light of the lording sky
An old blind man is with me where I go

Walking in the meadows of his son's eye
On whom a world of ills came down like snow.
He cried as he died, fearing at last the spheres'

Last sound, the world going out without a breath:
Too proud to cry, too frail to check the tears,
And caught between two nights, blindness and death.

O deepest wound of all that he should die
On that darkest day. Oh, he could hide
The tears out of his eyes, too proud to cry.

Until I die he will not leave my side.)

––––––––––––

This unfinished Elegy of Dylan Thomas was given the title
"Elegy" in the latest version of the poem after the provisional

titles "The Darkest Way" or "Too Proud to Die" or "True Death" had been used in preparatory drafts. Among his papers he left sixty pages of manuscript work towards the poem, including this note:—

(1) *Although he was too proud to die, he did die, blind, in the most agonizing way but he did not flinch from death & was brave in his pride.*

(2) *In his innocence, & thinking he was God-hating, he never knew that what he was was: an old kind man in his burning pride.*

(3) *Now he will not leave my side, though he is dead.*

(4) *His mother said that as a baby he never cried; nor did he, as an old man; he just cried to his secret wound & his blindness, never aloud.*

The rest of the manuscript work consists of phrases, lines, couplets, and line-endings, and transcripts of the poem in various degrees of completeness. The two more complete versions, which are clearly the latest, are both rhymed in quatrains. One, with no title, has no division into verses, and the second, with the title "Elegy," is divided into verses of three lines. This, to me, seems to be the latest version of all, and seems to hold the final form the poem was to take. The poem extends to the seventeenth line, ending "to the roots of the sea," after which there is a line which is deleted.

The extension of the poem has been built up from the manuscript's notes. The lines are all found there, except that two or three have been adjusted to fit the rhyming scheme. "Breath" was an isolated marginal word which I have used in line thirty-four; and "plain," which ends line twenty-three, has been added to "was" without justification from the manuscript. In the third line I have chosen "narrow pride" as against "burning pride" although "burning" occurs more often than "narrow" in the transcripts; but it was "narrow" in that line he quoted to me from memory when I last saw him.

Of the added lines sixteen are exactly as Dylan Thomas wrote them, and the remainder are altered only to the extent of an inversion of one or two words. Their order might well have been different. The poem might also have been made much longer. It recalls the earlier poem, also written for his father: "Do not go gentle into that good night"; but it is clear that in this last poem Dylan Thomas was attempting something even more immediate and more difficult.

VERNON WATKINS